HOW BIG SHOULD GOVERNMENT BE?

*First in the second series of Rational Debate Seminars
sponsored by the American Enterprise Institute
held at
The George Washington University
Washington, D. C.*

HOW BIG SHOULD GOVERNMENT BE?

Paul H. Douglas
and
J. Enoch Powell

Published by
American Enterprise Institute
for Public Policy Research

AEI's first Rational Debate of the 1967-68 academic year brought together two seasoned politicians skilled in sharp-tongued forensics. Former Senator Paul H. Douglas is one of this country's venerated liberals. His credentials include authorship of the Federal Social Security Act, the Area Redevelopment Act, the Economic Development Act, and many other laws throughout his 20 distinguished years in the United States Senate. He has been a leader in the fight for medicare, federal aid to education, civil rights, highway beautification, urban renewal, and tax reform. A war hero and an economist who has been president of the American Economic Association, Senator Douglas attained even more prominence as a politician.

J. Enoch Powell, a Greek scholar and a prolific author and poet, entered politics after an illustrious career in the British army during World War II. Like Senator Douglas, he quickly made a name for himself. But unlike the Senator, he ascended on the conservative side. He was a member of the British Tory cabinet and now serves as spokesman on defense matters in the shadow cabinet. The British parliamentary system, in which polemics are well-developed, spawns great debaters, and Mr. Powell ranks with the best.

Senator Douglas gave the first lecture. Anticipating an assault on large government expenditures, he analyzed government costs to demonstrate that reductions are not easy. Defense and its related costs, past and present, account for a major proportion of federal expenditures. The Senator also challenged what he called the "naive and erroneous assumptions of so many foes of government activity that public expenditures are in their very nature inherently wasteful and unproductive." On the contrary, he said, most government expenditures furnish goods and services that are desired by the public and that, therefore, from an economic point of view, must be regarded as desired products.

It is the conservatives, he counter-charged, who plunder the public treasury, while venting their anger on "welfare expenditures and on legislation designed to protect the weak and ignorant from the strong and cunning."

"The American conservatives tend to ignore or defend the direct and indirect subsidies to the airlines and the owners of private planes, to newspapers, magazines, and direct advertisers," the Illinois liberal said. "They are relatively oblivious to the big subsidies given to the ship-building and ship operators. They will not wish to curtail the space program or the supersonic air transport program. They will defend to the death the privilege granted to Congress by the Constitution, which we have nevertheless conferred upon the banks, of creating monetary purchasing power. Conservatives will continue to welcome governmental expenditures on irrigation and flood control, sending up the value of the land benefited. They are pleased to have the government subsidize their research, provided they can retain the patent rights. Their representatives amongst the big farmers oppose any limitation on farm subsidies to individuals. The big farmers will pocket their subsidies, which frequently run over $25,000 a year and sometimes over $1 million, and continue to beat down every effort to trim them."

Mr. Powell took a different and more philosophical approach, arguing that the question of "more or less government" was really a question about "sorts and methods of government." He concentrated on the nature of a society's decision-making process—on the characteristics of prescribed (government) and spontaneous (free market) decision-making systems and the scope given to these two systems within a society. Decisions by specific government, he maintained, are arbitrary, limited, and contain a strong element of national self-consciousness. These characteristics are exemplified in the extreme, he said, by attempts to win the race to the moon, or achieve a faster rate of economic growth than one's neighbors, at the cost of other uses for the same bundle of resources that might have given greater satisfaction. The closer a nation approaches the totalitarian model, he said, the bigger its drive to excel in the international "growthmanship" competition.

The British Tory leader observed that the U. S. had decreed huge and continuing expenditures on space research and astronautics "which may be in part, but are far from wholly, motivated by considerations of defense."

Then he asked: "Why does a government decide, like Pharaoh commanding the erection of a pyramid, that large slabs of the energy of its citizens shall be devoted to the specific end of putting a man on the moon or a probe on Venus?"

The British MP also castigated the government-planned economy as "immensely inferior" to a free market system in efficiency. Government economic decisions are necessarily poor, he said, because they are centralized and because they have to be made prematurely.

"Both these characteristics automatically exclude an enormous mass of information which the market is capable of digesting," he commented. "The market works continuously and receives impressions from any and every source: the processes of exploration, investigation, and decision are not separated but coincide. This is something which no system involving a centralized and conscious judgment can rival."

And, he added, "the market does not have to produce decisions too soon. . . . [It] does not have to decide in advance whether natural gas will be found in the North Sea, nor how much, nor what it will cost to exploit it." But a national economic plan for 1970 does, he pointed out, even though it cannot possibly know in advance what will happen.

Mr. Powell, first in rebuttal, pointed to nationalized medical care and arbitrary wage-setting, whether through minimum wage laws or union power, as clumsy means of seeking social objectives. A national medical-care system limits citizens to just that measure of attention established by the government, even though they may have wanted more: "In the absence of the [British] National Health Service more medical care, rather than less, would probably have got itself provided." Arbitrary wage-setting, he argued, unavoidably reduces the demand for labor and therefore increases unemployment—insofar as it is effective in raising wages above market levels. "Deliberate redistribution—such as family allowances—would be more efficient and would distort . . . the market less."

For his part, Senator Douglas thought his British adversary had far too much faith in the ability of the market system to remedy social and economic ills.

"I submit that if we have any concern for human values, we cannot take the market demands of the poor as an adequate measure of their basic human needs," Senator Douglas declared. "For this group has very little market demand since it has very little income. Without advocating equality of income, which I do not, some marked reduction in this disparity is called for. But it will not be obtained by market decisions which must take the existing distribution of income for granted. This disparity will not be greatly reduced by private philanthrophy, excellent as that may be and is. It can only be appreciably reduced through government policies of taxation and expenditure."

The arguments in the final session, with the seminar participants freely joining in, tended to center around two questions, whether the ballot box *in fact* corrects or reinforces the inequalities of the marketplace and whether the objective of income redistribution is served better by providing the poor with services or with income supplements .

HOW BIG SHOULD GOVERNMENT BE?

Paul H. Douglas
J. Enoch Powell

RATIONAL DEBATE SEMINARS

American Enterprise Institute
for Public Policy Research
Washington, D. C.

Library of Congress Catalog Number 68-19631

FOREWORD

With this vigorous and scholarly discussion on "How Big Should Government Be?" the American Enterprise Institute launches its second series of Rational Debates. We hope these confrontations between eminent men on great issues of the day will help to buttress our free society. As we explained in inaugurating these Rational Debates a little more than a year ago, public issues of vital importance to the nation are seldom simple, yet all too often they are discussed in absolute terms. The purpose of these debates is to present the grays as well as the blacks and whites, to learn about as many well-reasoned sides to a given problem as can be found.

In addition to the debate here presented, which features former Senator Paul H. Douglas and British Member of Parliament J. Enoch Powell, the American Enterprise Institute is presenting three other public policy debates during the 1967-68 academic year: "Educational TV: Who Should Pay?" with Ronald Coase and Edward W. Barrett; "Welfare Programs: An Economic Appraisal" featuring James Tobin and W. Allen Wallis; and "Fair Trial and Free Press" with Paul C. Reardon and Clifton Daniel.

In the 1966-67 academic year, AEI presented debates on the following topics: "Congress and the Presidency: Their Role in Modern Times," Arthur M. Schlesinger, Jr., and Alfred de Grazia; "Law, Order and Civil Disobedience," Charles E. Whittaker and William Sloane Coffin, Jr.; "Full Employment, Guideposts and Economic Stability," Arthur F. Burns and Paul A. Samuelson; and "The Balance of Payments: Free Versus Fixed Exchange Rates," Milton Friedman and Robert V. Roosa.

AEI's purpose in these debates, as in its other activities since its founding in 1943, is to produce research, publications, seminars, and symposia to help legislators, policymakers, educators, the press, and the general public reach informed judgments on major questions of the day.

February 16, 1968   William J. Baroody
                      President
                      American Enterprise Institute
                          for Public Policy Research

PREFACE

In this lively encounter opening the second series of Rational Debates, Senator Paul H. Douglas and the Honorable J. Enoch Powell engage in a dialogue on one of the critical issues of the day. Their task was to set forth two opposing cases on how big government should be, revealing concisely and clearly the basic areas of disagreement on fact and philosophy. They have done so with elegance and dispatch.

The debate took place in three sessions before a select group of academicians, newsmen, and government officials. It is reproduced here as it happened, so that the public may now witness the presentations, rebuttals, and interchange between speakers and audience.

Once again, the American Enterprise Institute is to be commended for its contribution toward intelligent discussion of current issues of public policy.

February 15, 1968

G. Warren Nutter
Coordinator
Rational Debate Series

CONTENTS

FIRST LECTURE

PAUL H. DOUGLAS

In 1965-66, total governmental expenditures in this country, federal, state, and local, amounted to $225 billion[1] or approximately 30 percent of the gross national product of $743 billion and 37 percent of the total national income of $610 billion for 1966. This seems to be an enormous amount and certainly it is a very large one. Before we pass judgment upon it, however, we should analyze it a bit more closely. About $5 billion or nearly 2 percent of the total was spent on government pensions and probably should not be included among the expenditures for current goods and services.

It will surprise many that a full three-sevenths of the total, or over $97 billion, was spent by state and local governments, not by the federal government. The percentage spent by the state and local governments is appreciably larger, of course, than the sums collected by state and local governments because of federal aid which is given to the states.

Similarly, because of the system of federal aid and state aid, the farther down you go, the amounts spent by the lower levels of government, if one may use that phrase, as compared to the amounts raised by local units of government, increases. This percentage spent by state and local governments has been rapidly increasing throughout the last 20 years. Those who customarily attack the federal government as the main source for the increase in total governmental expenditures should therefore look closer to home.

But I should like to challenge immediately the naive and erroneous assumptions of so many foes of government activity that public expenditures are in their very nature inherently wasteful and unproductive. On the contrary, the vast proportion of government expenditures are directed to the furnishing of goods and services which the public desires and which from an economic point of view must be regarded as desired products. Many billions also constitute capital investments for the future. If we had followed the practice of private corporations, such as AT&T, and had not included these capital investments in our operating budgets, then for nearly all the postwar years with the exception of 1957-58 and 1966-67, there would have been no operating deficit.

Also, let me point out that the biggest civilian outlay is for education, which in 1965-66 took $35 billion. This was about 5 percent of the gross national product and 6 percent of the national income. Now I am aware of the fact that historically the British Tories and Conservatives have been lukewarm or hostile to the idea of public education for the people and have in general tried first to oppose and then to stint it. That is precisely what many conservatives in this country would like to do.

I am happy, however, that this is not the attitude of the vast majority of the American people. They have believed, and correctly, that education makes men and women more productive than they would otherwise be, helps them to be wiser citizens and makes life itself richer and more worthwhile. American education has many faults but it is certainly one reason for the great surge forward of this country in material prosperity, while the class limitations on education in Great Britain, fostered and maintained by the conservative elements, have operated to hold back the industrial advance of that great nation.

I do not think that conservative opposition, however plausibly presented, will induce the American people to give up needed training for their sons and daughters. Nor should it. If I may ignore elementary and secondary education for the time being, which, of course, is much more important than higher education, remember that 40 years ago there was a ratio of about one university student in Great Britain for each thousand of the population. We at that time had an average of four or five to the thousand. Now the British average is four or five to the thousand but our average is perhaps 25 to the thousand. I am not speaking about the quality of education. Our English friends will maintain that their quality is superior. I am simply speaking of the quantitative aspects of the education.

The second great source of state and local expenditures is highways, upon which $13 billion was spent in 1965-66. I admit that at times I have wondered if we were not putting too much money in those ribbons of concrete. But every time I tried in the Senate to cut the federal grants-in-aid for this purpose, I found myself overpowered by the indignant opposition of the prosperous conservative and business interests of the nation. They liked the highways to ride on and felt that more were always needed so that they could take longer journeys and live farther out from the metropolitan centers. More highways, they believed, were also necessary so that the automobile industry could grow, more oil and gas could be purchased, and the cement industry could thrive. In the process the contractors and allied trades would also prosper.

A third important service furnished by government is that of police and fire protection, on which we spent $5 billion in 1966-67. Even Adam Smith would not question this, as evidenced in his essay on *Justice, Police and Arms*. Police and fire departments paid for by voluntary subscriptions or by donated time, such as those which Ben Franklin started in the early eighteenth century in Philadelphia, proved themselves inferior to professional services furnished and financed by the state. Volunteer departments were superceded by the middle of the nineteenth century. (If it is not heresy in these quarters, you should read Sidney and Beatrice Webb's volumes on the evolution of local government.) We in the United States have not gone as far, however, as the British Conservative party in this respect. For it was the great Tory leader, Sir Robert Peel, who nationalized the British police forces. That incidentally is why the British policemen are called Bobbies, and, sometimes, Peelers. We have therefore not gone as far as Mr. [J. Enoch] Powell's party and we do not intend to do so. For we believe that police and fire protection should be primarily local functions. We are not in favor of building up a *staats polizei*. However, let me make it clear that the nationalized British police force is in no sense like the Nazi and Russian secret police and that the liberties of Britons have not been eroded by its existence.

Another billion dollars of public money goes for jails and prisons. I often think these could be improved, but I notice that conservatives never urge that they be abandoned. On the contrary, they often want to add to the number of their inmates as an alleged deterrent to crime.

We spend locally for sewage, garbage collection, and street cleaning approximately $3 billion. England resolved not to tolerate the garbage-laden streets and the filth of Henry Fielding's England. We have tried to follow suit. I cannot believe that even the doctrinaire opponents of government spending would seriously propose giving this up. In order to prevent pollution of air and water, we will have to spend in the future much more rather than less. We do not want to go through that black week which killed 4,000 fine Englishmen in and around London by the poisonous smog, and which also caused great loss of life in Donora, Pennsylvania.

This brings us to health and hospitals. The British and European conservatives have never been very strong for these outlays. Despite the discoveries of Pasteur in the field of bacteriology and of Joseph Lister in the field of antiseptic surgery, British and Continental medicine and hospitals have lagged badly behind our levels of achievement. We could perhaps further improve our work but few would begrudge the $8 billion we now spend on health and hospitals. These outlays help to prolong life, reduce pain, and deepen the enjoyment which comes from better health. The only difficulty is that these measures are still relatively unavailable to the poor and to those with lower incomes. Let our opponents, if they dare, propose to cut down on these items. Let Mr. Powell, if he proposes to put America on what he regards as a sound footing, propose to reduce these appropriations for health and hospitals. We will lock horns with him if he does.

One of the biggest items of governmental expense is, of course, interest on the public debt. We spent $12 billion for that purpose in 1965-66, and there will be more this year. Three-quarters of this was an outlay by the federal government on its debt of $320 billion. Of this, $231 billion or 70 percent of the total was incurred as a result of World Wars I and II and the Korean War. Would our conservative friends repudiate those wars or suggest that we should not pay interest on the debts we incurred in fighting them?

Next on the list comes the postal service, which I have charged with its total expenditures of $5.6 billion rather than with its real deficit of close to a billion dollars. In spite of all criticism, the post office is handling well over 70 billion pieces of mail a year. It does so with compara- tive efficiency considering the bad handwriting with which it has to deal and the huge territory which it has to cover. I doubt if private industry could do as well. If it were put on a purely profit-making basis, virtually all third and fourth class post offices would probably have to be closed down because they operate at a loss, and all rural routes would have to be discontinued because they operate at a loss. Either that or the rates would have to be raised for these localities. Can one imagine the uproar which would be created by such a policy? There would be a strong demand that we return to the present system of equality of service regardless of residence.

Throughout my Senate career I was, however, dis- tressed by the size of the postal deficit—which, after stripping away some disingenuous bookkeeping would run between three-quarters of a billion and a billion dollars a year. It was not hard to find out where the losses were. They were not on first class mail or the ordinary letter and postcard. This type of mail actually yielded a surplus. The real deficits came instead from second and third class mail with an assist from fourth class. Second class mail consists of newspapers and magazines. When

I last saw the figures they were only paying about 27 percent of their mailing cost and were being indirectly subsidized by the taxpayers to the tune of about $350 million a year. Another $350 million was being lost on third class mail, the unsealed matter called "junk mail" which clutters up the wastebaskets of the nation. Direct mail advertising, hair oil, toothpaste, and other samples are sent out third class. Some of us, including Congressman Rhodes of Pennsylvania, Senator Proxmire of Wisconsin, and myself, tried for years to make second and third class mail self-supporting by increasing its rates and thus getting it off the backs of the American taxpayer. What a going over we received! The magazines and newspapers which trumpeted from every editorial their opposition to government deficits and subsidies rose in outrage against this effort and defeated it. So did the direct mail advertisers, whose representatives furnish a respectable component of every advertising club in the nation and who at the luncheons with their fellows cheer to the echo all proposals to cut the federal budget and eliminate those feeding from the public trough.

I hope that when our good British friend tours the country to expound his opposition to subsidies he will not confine himself to ideological gatherings but will do as I did for over a decade—namely, carry the battle into the advertising clubs of the nation and discuss the question of self-supporting postal rates for second, third, and fourth class mail.

I have long felt that we were spending too much on

the dredging of rivers and harbors and what is called the "pork barrel." Many of these expenditures, in providing lakes, etc., are beneficial, but many are very wasteful. I waged a discriminating war on these outlays for over a decade, but I never received any help from the conservative block in Congress or in the country. On the contrary, it was the business groups which initiated, promoted, and carried through these projects. Much the same was true of the irrigation projects on the upper Colorado River, where we are irrigating land at a height of many thousands of feet at a cost, including interest, of over $1,000 an acre in order to grow potatoes and apples in short seasons and raise the value of the land by about $100 per acre.

We are also subsidizing private planes for the wealthy and powerful by permitting them to use public fields for a very inadequate charge. Friends of mine who have studied this issue report that the hidden subsidy is not far from $125 million. We are also bearing heavy costs for the development of a supersonic plane which can only be used by the international jet set at the cost of shattering the eardrums and nerves of millions of the earthbound who cannot afford to take peregrinations in the skies.

Even urban renewal got into the act. It was originally designed to help the poor. At least I thought it was, because I was the floor manager for that section of the bill in 1949 when it was first passed by Congress. But the billions already spent and to be spent are being used predominantly to write down the cost of slum land so that not only civil amenities may be encouraged but also subsidies may be given to commercial institutions and the well-to-do, who alone can live in the high-rise and garden apartments for the wealthy which rise on the former slums of the poor. It has been a bonanza for certain groups in the population but it has not focused on helping the low-income groups of the cities whom many of us thought we were going to help when we promoted its passage. This failure of urban renewal to aid the poor was one factor which helped to create the disastrous riots in New Haven, Detroit, and certain other cities last summer. There were many reasons for those riots. But certainly one reason was the feeling on the part of the poor, particularly the poor Negroes, that they had been left out in the plans which had been drawn and carried through for the improvement of the cities. Newark was another example of this feeling.

It is significant that the former powerful opponents of urban renewal have by now largely disappeared from the national scene. Urban renewal grants now sail through Congress with little, if any, opposition and an almost audible smacking of lips.

I do not know whether our British friend disapproves of public libraries upon which we spend a half billion a year. In times past, the Conservatives did oppose them, but libraries are now accepted as part of continuing education. I think the libraries are highly civilizing institutions and that life in many cities and towns would be arid and barren without them. In times past, Great Britain was very neglectful of its *Jude the Obscures,* described by Thomas Hardy, who hungered and thirsted after knowledge and to whom all doors were closed. I may say that I read an interesting article on William Blake a few months ago. You remember that Blake spoke of the "dark satanic mills" of England. I always thought he referred to the factories. But the students of Blake now say that he was referring to Oxford and Cambridge, as the dark satanic mills where students were mistrained and the poor were not allowed to get an education. Britain is doing much better today and the local Laborites and Liberals deserve most of the credit for it.

Local parks are a similar amenity upon which we spend nearly $1.25 billion a year. To many of those who have broad country estates or who are able to take vacations in the Caribbean or the wilds of Canada, this seems like a wasteful extravagance. When I was an alderman in Chicago, I encountered an underground movement which would have sold off some of our great lake-shore parks for upper-income housing. But its supporters never quite dared to surface. For they knew the public cherished these bits of beautiful open space, that the parks gave to hard-pressed millions a sense of spaciousness and of a relaxed life closer to nature which was very precious to them. I am not ashamed of being for public parks, as well as libraries, and I challenge our British friend to prove that his 50 million countrymen and our 200 million Americans can acquire satisfactory private parks of their own. This is certainly one of many illustrations where individual needs can only be satisfied by collective action.

But I am not only for local parks. I am for national parks as well. Anyone who has been in the national parks of Yellowstone, Glacier, and the Grand Canyon would not think of selling them off unless he were the most selfish of Philistines. One of the great men of this country was Frederick Law Olmsted, who was responsible for some of the great city and national parks. He wrote the best book on the South prior to the Civil War. He journeyed through the slave states, and was head of the sanitary commission during the Civil War. After the war he was a great landscape gardener for Central Park, Jackson and Washington Parks in Chicago, the park system in Boston, and a whole series of other parks. There is need for further action to save beautiful open spaces which are being steadily gobbled up and defaced by private industry. The Indiana Dunes near Chicago are an example. Some of us have been waging a ten-year battle to save that area for the people, and at every turn our opponents have been the powerful conservatives and business leaders who want to ring Lake Michigan with a solid wall of steel mills and power plants, belching as they now do waste into the lake, polluting the air, and shutting off the people from its shores.

I submit that the approximately $1 billion a year which the national government spends on its parks, forests, public lands, and for other outdoor purposes is on the whole money well spent. There are powerful private interests seeking to despoil these lands by overgrazing, by the predatory cutting of timber and, most of all at the moment, by trying to take over the incredibly rich oil shale deposits in the Western slope of the Central Rockies. I hope that our British friend, as he travels over the country, will not inadvertently strengthen their hands or weaken the hands of those who are struggling against heavy odds to protect the priceless public resources of oil shale. The figures there are incredible. The Geological Survey estimates that the oil content of the shale lands in northwestern Colorado, eastern Utah, and southwestern Wyoming come to two trillion barrels. And that is not a slip of either tongue or pen, two trillion barrels, which at the price of $2.75 a barrel would be worth five and one-half trillions of dollars, 80 percent of which is, for the moment, in public ownership. Whether we can hold it or not is another story.

Incidentally a visitor to the national parks cannot help but notice that very few of the poor or low-income groups visit the parks. The patrons are almost exclusively members of the upper middle-class who can afford the costs of a long automobile journey. This emphasizes the need for parks close to the teeming metropolitan centers of population. I am happy to say that Mr. Laurance Rockefeller has seen this need in a most public-spirited fashion and has been working to meet it. It is also proper to point out that he is carrying on the tradition of his father John D. Rockefeller, Jr., who was almost solely responsible for buying and giving to the government the great parks of the Grand Tetons, the Great Smokies, Mt. Desert in Maine, and who carried out the restoration of Colonial Williamsburg. I hope the example of the Rockefeller family in this respect may be more widely copied.

When Mr. Powell and others bewail the large outlays of the federal government, they should direct their attention to war as the chief cause for the expenditures. Past wars are directly responsible for 70 percent of the existing federal debt, or as I have said about $231 billion, and for most of the $12.5 billion in interest which was paid out in 1965-66. War has been indirectly responsible for the expenditure by us of nearly $100 billion in our postwar efforts to help the war-crippled countries and people of the world. About $17 billion of this was an outright donation to Great Britain and to the democracies of Western Europe. I felt it was my duty to support these grants. Would Mr. Powell oppose our making them, or would he merely say our total expenditures were too high without specifying these items which it would have been very easy for us to have cut or discontinued. We have reaped little goodwill from these expenditures. On the contrary, it often seems that the more we do for foreign governments and people, the more enemies we make among those whom we have tried to help. The most striking illustration of this fact is, of course, General Charles de Gaulle, the President and leader of France, who has sought to repay our wartime and postwar help with a determined effort to undermine us economically and weaken us politically. If there should be a revival of isolationism and a withdrawal of the United States from the world in an attempt to live within Fortress America, which there may well be, we will have General de Gaulle, more than any other man, to thank for it. If that happens, will he and his followers then be pleased with their efforts? Will the sincere lovers of both peace and freedom who have heaped attacks on us from both Asia and Europe look back upon their work and call it good?

These outlays for foreign aid of well over $100 billion, are, however, merely peripheral consequences of war. The main costs of war, of course, lie within the Department of Defense itself. Defense expenditures amounted to nearly $60 billion in 1965-66, and they will reach at least $70 billion in the current budget and possibly more. In 1965-66 the outlay of $60 billion was about one half of all federal expenditures—it is *over* one half this year—and nearly 30 percent of all governmental outlays, federal, state, and local. Since World War II, we have probably spent for defense close to three-quarters of a trillion dollars, enough to have made this country an earthly paradise which would have satisfied even William Blake. Due to the war in Vietnam and the efforts of the Communists to take over Southeast Asia, we are now spending $70 billion a year.

I do not know what Mr. Powell would have us do about these expenditures. But the Conservative frame of mind has never been hostile to military expenditures in the past. Nor, with the exception of a few men such as Lord Robert Cecil, have the Conservatives been devoted to the cause of world peace. They have tended instead to be "hard-liners," imperialists who believed in the "white man's burden" and dominance over what their favorite poet Kipling called the "lesser breeds without the law." Imperialism, which was dominant during the decade from 1895 to 1905, helped to get the world into the mess we are now in. I am one of those who believe in peace *with* freedom. In fact, I believe that without freedom we cannot have peace for long. I was, therefore, opposed to the aggression of the Nazis and I want to congratulate the British for their heroic resistance which fortunately became general among the Western world.

I am equally opposed, and so is the American government, to Communist aggression, and this is the primary reason why we are in South Vietnam. We are not seeking conquest or domination, but merely the right of the Vietnamese and other peoples to develop free governments and institutions instead of being engulfed by an all-powerful police state. The going is rough. Our costs are heavy. The struggle takes place far away. But it is important. For if we are forced by military pressure and domestic disaffection to withdraw from South Vietnam, we will probably have to withdraw from all of Southeastern Asia. It would then seem inevitable that these countries would come under the control of a Communist police state with a loss of millions of lives. And what then about India?

While I have great respect for the sincere non-resistants and for their faith in the infectious power of energized goodwill, and while I believe this spirit has a real place both in the relationships between individuals and between democratic states, there are just not enough people who would practice this when faced with a power like Nazi Germany or Communist Russia or China to make it possible as a national policy. Since any resistance would be belated, it would be ineffective. Moreover, a police state, by its control of terror and propaganda, would prevent such an appeal from taking root among its own members.

Heavy as the human and economic costs of the war are, therefore, I submit that in all probability it would ultimately be worse if we were now to pull out under pressure from South Vietnam. Many in Asia and Europe will admit this privately but at the same time refuse to give us any public encouragement. In the analogy of Aesop, they are all for letting us "bell the cat." I take it you all know this story of Aesop—or perhaps this generation didn't grow up on Aesop's fables. The mice were worried by the cat. The cat was making depredations amongst them. So they gathered together in conference to decide what they would do. They finally decided they would tie a bell around the neck of the cat. They unanimously agreed on this.

Then one mouse asked, "Well, who will bell the cat?" There was silence, and the assembly of the mice dissolved. Let me, therefore, take this opportunity to thank the

Labor government of Great Britain for the general support which they have given us in this crisis. Mr. Powell, please hear. It has been hard for the Labor government to support the United States' Vietnam policy in the face of the general anti-American sentiment among the British people. We know this and appreciate their attitude the more because of it.

But war has created other expenses, such as the nearly $5 billion for veterans services. Perhaps some economies could be made here but on the whole the public properly believes that we should help care for men who have risked their lives, or are ready to risk their lives, in the nation's service. I cannot believe that our British friend would have us shirk this moral duty. If we include interest on the war debt, veterans costs, and foreign military aid, the direct war costs will run close to $84 billion, or a strong three-fifths of all federal governmental outlays.

Atomic energy and the exploration of space are by-products of war. They are in part pursued for military purposes and partly are involved in the struggle for comparative prestige. Together they consume about $10 billion a year. I have some very strong reservations on the space race. But does our friend advise that we pull out of both these competitions? I would certainly give up the effort to put a man on the moon by 1970 or 1972. That will have no military value nor any real scientific value. And what is the use of getting there first, if there is no use in getting there at all? If atomic energy and space exploration costs are added to military costs, the total will amount to $94 billion—or about 70 percent of federal expenses and over 40 percent of all governmental expenditures, federal, state, and local. It is, therefore, the warfare world and not the welfare state which keeps government expenditures up and taxes high. The problem of world peace is therefore central.

I think I can predict nevertheless where most conservatives, American or British, think we are spending too much and where the state should curtail its activities. This is on welfare expenditures and on legislation designed to protect the weak and ignorant from the strong and cunning.

The American conservatives tend to ignore or defend the direct and indirect subsidies to the airlines and the owners of private planes, to newspapers, magazines, and direct advertisers. They are relatively oblivious to the big subsidies given to the shipbuilding and ship operators. They will not wish to curtail the space program or the supersonic air transport program. They will defend to the death the privilege granted to Congress by the Constitution, which we have nevertheless conferred upon the banks, of creating monetary purchasing power. Conservatives will continue to welcome governmental expenditures on irrigation and flood control, sending up the value of the land benefitted. They are pleased to have the government subsidize their research, provided they can retain the patent rights. Their representatives amongst the big farmers oppose any limitation on farm subsidies to individuals. The big farmers will pocket their subsidies, which frequently run over $25,000 a year and sometimes over $1 million, and continue to beat down every effort to trim them.

Similarly they will continue to rally in defense of the depletion allowances on oil and gas and other sub-surface deposits, including depletion of oyster shells and clam shells, sand and gravel. These cost the taxpayers several billion dollars a year. Having obtained lower rates for capital gains, conservatives will successfully prevent even this tax from becoming fully operative by letting death wipe out the possibility of taxing all previous gains. They seem to think that wages and salaries should be treated more roughly in the reporting and collection of income taxes than dividends and interest. In short most, although fortunately not all, are quite anxious for special privileges for themselves, their associates, and their friends. General Eisenhower's final warning about the dangers to this country of "the military-industrial complex" fell on deaf ears and is almost forgotten today.

But what does arouse their ire are the welfare grants to the poor, the aged, the disabled, and especially the hard-pressed mothers with families of dependent children. It is the $4.7 billion of welfare payments and the nearly $2.2 billion of special aid under the so-called war on poverty which most excites them. It is this 1 percent of the gross national product which seems particularly heinous to them and not the much larger subsidies for the well-to-do. Whenever some financial emergency comes up, there-

fore, it is this group of expenditures which they first
want to cut or eliminate. Every slip by some hapless
worker in these programs is avidly noted and played up.

I found this group to be relatively indifferent to excessive expenditures for materials and contracts when I
waged war upon these abuses in the 1960s. They would
become indignant about the over-staffing of government
offices, as I was myself, but they showed no indignation
that there were 25 or so individuals with annual incomes
over $500,000 who paid no taxes at all and that a man
could have an economic income of $26 million and still
avoid all taxes. Nor would they seem to object to businesses getting outrageous prices for common tools such
as screwdrivers which, as I remember it, I purchased for
15 cents retail but which cost the government, as I remember it, about $2 wholesale. Nor would they seem to
object to firms making excess grossly profits in supplying
articles for the defense of the nation.

As I watched their political spokesmen operate during
my 18 years in the Senate, I found their reactions to be
almost visceral. If any proposal was designed to help the
poor and the weak, there would be a red flush of anger,
and a flow from the adrenal glands, and then an attack
upon the proposal as wasteful class legislation, as helping
to undermine individual initiative and the principle of
sturdy self-reliance. Almost any proposal to help the
well-to-do and the economically powerful would be
supported by these spokesmen as sound economics, while

attempts to limit such expenditures would be treated as demagogy.

The same standards of behavior have been applied in the case of regulatory legislation and practices. While the case for so-called free enterprise rests primarily on competition and not on monopoly, this distinction has never seemed to penetrate the minds of the opponents of all regulation. They have been bitterly opposed to the effective regulation of private monopolies, as in the case of the price of oil and gas at the wellhead. Moreover, they were either lethargic or opposed to legislation which would enable consumers to know what they were buying, as in the case of drugs or the terms for consumer credit. These are the fields where great abuses have prevailed and where the truth is easily concealed. But when some of us did battle so that borrowers could know what the real interest rates they were paying, and so that consumers might know the truth about precisely what was inside the bright packages they bought, we faced an almost solid front of business opposition.

Abraham Lincoln in his Baltimore speech of over a century ago spoke of the two theories of liberty—namely those of the wolf and of the sheep. The protection of the sheep, he pointed out, interfered with the liberty of the wolf and was resented by the pack but it was necessary to preserve the liberty of the sheep.

I am not condemning the top dogs of society as being primarily predators or wolves. There are many admirable and constructive men and women among them and our society would be far poorer without them. But there are also some predators and unless society wishes to abandon the weak to them, it must seek to protect the weak from them. Only the social Darwinians who believe that life is indeed red with tooth and claw will support an unrestricted struggle in which, as in the African jungle, the strong can freely prey and feed upon the weak.

I do not suppose that our British friend will say that our efforts to help the poor and unfortunate are contrary to American principles and are therefore basically un-American. Many of his associates, however, and I think Mr. Powell himself, believe that the welfare legislation initiated in 1911 by the British liberals under the leadership of Lloyd George and Winston Churchill and greatly extended by the Labor party from 1945 to 1951 under Clement Atlee are un-British. Many in the United States have attacked our Social Security Act of 1935 and the welfare legislation of John Kennedy and Lyndon Johnson as contrary to the American tradition.

Let me briefly deal with this question of tradition. The preamble to the Declaration of Independence declared in 1776 that foremost among the innate rights of man were those of "life, liberty, and the pursuit of happiness" and that "to secure these rights, governments are instituted amongst men deriving their just powers from the consent of the governed." In other words, governments are charged with the duty of helping men to pursue happiness, to chase it even if they might not catch it. If there ever was an affirmation that government should work to promote human welfare, that was it.

The newly independent states were quick to see and affirm this faith. The Articles of Confederation under which the United States was governed until 1787 explicitly affirmed the "general welfare" as one of the fundamental purposes of the union. This was re-emphasized in the Constitution itself. For not only did the preamble make the promotion of the general welfare one of the basic purposes of the new republic, but in Article I, Section 8, the general welfare was again affirmed as one of the purposes for which Congress could levy and spend taxes.

Finally, in Lincoln's Gettysburg Address, which has become the modern statement of the American faith, he spoke of our government being one "of the people, *by* the people, and *for* the people." All governments— whether tyrannies, aristocracies, or democracies—are governments of the people. But what is essential to the American system is that ours is also *by* the people, and *for* the people.

Instead of power coming down from above through king and nobility, which was the prevailing faith in the Britain of George III and the France of Louis XV (and to which our good British friend seems to hold today when he describes the power of royalty and the majesty of the Crown, as the cement holding Great Britain together), our country was founded in the faith that power resided in the people and came up from them. Government was their creature and existed to serve them. The victory of this idea on the battlefields was a notable achievement. It was no accident that when the British fife and drum corps marched dejectedly out of Yorktown as Cornwallis surrendered, it played dolefully "The World Turned Upside Down."

Yes, it was indeed being turned upside down and the new faith was conquering the hearts of men and not merely their bodies. Within a little over a century even Britain adopted our philosophy. Yesterday that faith victoriously withstood the attacks of the Nazi police state. Today it confronts the attempts of the Communist police state to take over first Asia and then the world. Unless undermined from within by extremists at both ends of the political spectrum, it will survive this greatest test of all. But it will do so only if we show that we really believe in the principle that people are full-fledged *members* of the state and not *subjects* of the state. This is very hard for those who have been brought up in the tradition of rule by King and nobility to accept, as has been shown in the case of the British Tories. But it is not hard for us if we only understand the true American tradition.

Forty years ago when I spent many pleasant weeks in England, I would frequently go to the edifices of the Established Church where there would be sung the sonorous hymn, with organ music, glorifying class differentiation:

> The rich man in his castle,
> The poor man at the gate,
> God made them high and lowly,
> And ordered their estate.

Happily England has progressed greatly since then. It is becoming more American with every year. But let us not retrogress from the faith of Thomas Jefferson, Abraham Lincoln, and of the patriots who created and preserved American liberties. Let us not be led by siren voices to return to the doctrines against which we fought at Bunker Hill and which were defeated at Saratoga and Yorktown.

The truth of the matter is that as population and the pressure upon space increases, so does the need for ground rules to govern the relationships of men to each other. There is little need for traffic rules in the heart of the Maine woods, but people and vehicles could not move along Fifth Avenue without them. When men raised their own vegetables and their wheat and corn, and when they killed their own meat, there was no need for pure food laws. But when Upton Sinclair told the truth about the Chicago stock yards, even that sturdy individualist, Theodore Roosevelt, became convinced. And following this, Harvey Wiley, *Colliers Weekly,* and the Women's Clubs of America were able to begin protecting consumers from injurious drugs as well as injurious foods. Individual knowledge was just too inadequate to enable people to protect themselves. Efforts to protect the consumer in these respects have met with a great deal of

opposition as those of you who have read Morton
Mintz's book on the Food and Drug Administration
under Mr. Larrick and preceding administrations probably know.

Were we wrong in 1892 and 1913-14 in passing the
Sherman and Clayton Acts to preserve the self-regulating
qualities of true and ethical competition from being
smothered by the unfair and the monopolistic practices
of others? And if the followers of Mr. Powell appeal to
Adam Smith and Nassau William Senior as supporters
of their position, may I suggest that they also study Joan
Robinson's *The Economics of Imperfect Competition*
and Edward Chamberlin's book on *Monopolistic Competition?* It is a source of great disappointment to me that
Great Britain, which led the world in the enunciation of
the principles of competition, should have departed so
far from the actual practice of competition. Everywhere in Great Britain you see either closely-held monopolies or combinations of a small number of firms endeav-
oring to maintain prices higher than competitive prices
and thereby to restrict output. They have one chemical
company, I think two brewing companies, two chocolate
and cocoa companies, five banks. If you read Walter
Bagehot's book on Lombard Street, you read of an enormous number of country banks for which the London
banks acted as correspondents. Those were gobbled up
one by one. The economists of the country stood by
and made no protest. Long before the British national-

ized steel, steel was in the hands of a relatively small number of companies.

I once called the roll of the British industries and found that in nearly every industry competition had been largely superseded by cartels. And Mr. J. M. Keynes, who saw in higher-than-competitive interest rates one of the causes for the endemic unemployment in Great Britain, really missed the point. The cartelization of British industry, which he helped, was to my mind largely responsible for maintaining prices above the competitive level with a consequent choking off of demand and employment. So he helped to create the evil about which he wrote. And British industry not only acquiesced in this, but it cooperated most heartily. They called it rationalization.

Similarly, the scandalous practices of issuing stocks and bonds in the United States during the 1920s led to the reforms of the 1930s which, as I have said, were so bitterly opposed by the financial and business world. This battle is by no means over.

Those in England who have read the books by the Hammonds on the conditions of work in the mines and mills of Britain, and who have even a superficial acquaintanceship with Booth's *Life and Labour of the People of London* and Seebohm Rowntree's study of *Poverty in York* should know that the protective legislation passed by Liberals and Labor over the opposition of the Conservatives as led by Lord Salisbury, Arthur Balfour, and Sir Michael Hicks Beach was necessary and beneficial. Can those who have been so consistently wrong in the past be implicitly accepted as being right in the present?

Before we impatiently reject the Fair Labor Standards Act, let us read again the Brandeis-Goldmark briefs in support of the origin of the Oregon and District of Columbia Minimum Wage Laws and the Oregon 10- and 8-hour day laws. And let us realize that the same siren calls of opposition were heard in the past from the most respectable of sources such as Nicholas Murray Butler, the former prestigious President of Columbia University.

Ignorance and weakness not only handicap the ignorant and the weak, but they also handicap their children and thus help to intensify the cumulative cycle of poverty. In the process, ability and talents will be choked off which might otherwise function not only for the benefit of their possessors but for that of the human race as well.

Similarly the individual adult workman, when standing alone, was and is no match for the average large employer. His own wages were low and his savings meager or nonexistent. There were many unemployed all about him. It was more important for him to get a job than for the employer to hire him to fill one. Consequently he stood at a great disadvantage when he bargained with the employers. As a result he could be forced to accept disadvantageous terms which, in turn, tended to become cumulatively self-perpetuating. And when the workers tried to form unions, they could be discharged with impunity.

In 1935, Congress passed one of the most bitterly opposed acts of all time: the Wagner Labor Relations Act. This provided (1) that men should not be discriminated against because of union membership or activity and (2) that if in a free and fair election, a majority of the workers in a given bargaining unit chose to be represented by a given union, then it was the duty of the employer to sit down in good faith around a bargaining table and try to reach an agreement. The employer did not have to reach an agreement. He could reject the demands of the union. But he must at least negotiate in good faith in trying to reach an agreement. In the words of Woodrow Wilson, "permanent processes" for industrial peace were to be opened up.

The interpretation and carrying out of these principles naturally has created many difficulties, both of policy and enforcement. But I submit they are essentially sound and instead of being rejected need to be implemented. By so doing men will be enabled to help protect themselves collectively instead of relying upon the state. Properly interpreted, the Wagner Act is therefore an agency for the democratic decentralization of power instead of its concentration in either ownership or the state.

Similarly, in recent times we have contracted many of the service functions of government out to private bodies. Thus private organizations were the contractors for both the construction and management of the atomic energy plants at Oak Ridge and Hanford. Universities have taken over the management of the Argonne, Brookhaven, and Livermore facilities of the Atomic Energy Commission. Private organizations operate most of the Job Corps camps and centers financed by the Office of Economic Opportunity. Credit unions have been encouraged by the government to help create a constructive substitute for the loan shark.

In housing, the government no longer insists on huge publicly-owned and managed housing projects. It is ready to lease homes for individuals, pay rent supplements to nonprofit-making groups, and allow private industry latitude in building and managing such decentralized public housing as is authorized. In these ways, power can be decentralized and individual energies fostered. Let not the honorable conservatives tear down the pillars of the homes which many would like to demolish.

Finally, let me add a few words about the necessity for preserving individual freedom in a world of giant organizations. I think I am as sensitive as anyone can be to the danger that an all-powerful state can compel uniformity in action and in thought and that it can use its powers of terror and propaganda to suppress dissent. The experience with the police states should convince us all of this very fact. And for those who can learn only from literature rather than from life, may I urge all to read Aldous Huxley's *Brave New World* (where the geneticists were in control), Arthur Koestler's *Darkness at Noon,* and George Orwell's *Animal Farm* and his *1984.*

While meeting the common needs which I have out-lined, the powers of the central government can be dis-tributed among smaller units by grants-in-aid to the states and, as I have mentioned, by contract. The indi-vidual can and should be protected by intermediate socie-ties such as unions and professional associations, churches, and organizations such as the Civil Liberties Union. Rival political parties should be encouraged and maintained. Elected representatives should take on the task of helping to prevent individuals from being victimized by the bureaucracy and how they can do that! The independent grievance representatives modeled on the Swedish Om-budsman would be a further healthy protection.

But freedom is not menaced by the state alone. Big corporations can and frequently do exercise a similar control over their executives and employees. Here one does not get ahead by getting out of step. To get ahead, one customarily has to go along. The result is a substan-tial degree of forced uniformity of belief among the office employees which in nonunion firms can extend among the blue-collar workers as well. Company towns tend to be intolerant of differences. Industrial surveil-lance and espionage have been quite common in the past and certainly exist in the present. Recently we have seen the way in which one huge company tried to intim-idate and smear a courageous young engineer who was trying to protect the lives and limbs of the American public. We have come to grant the necessity for aca-demic freedom. We similarly need the pledge and practice of corporate and industrial freedom. At a time when computers are centralizing information about individuals and electronic devices can make surveillance all-pervasive, the effective rights to privacy need to be asserted. Those who attack the beneficent activities of the state should at least join us in defending these rights to privacy, whethe.· they be threatened by the state or corporation, whether by political parties or industrial hierarchies. Thus far the response from the business community, to put it mildly, has not been overwhelming.

It is, I believe, both appropriate and necessary that I should clear up some of the misconceptions which many of our opponents seem to entertain about our attitude towards state enterprise and which some of their numbers assiduously spread. We are not Socialists. We believe that competitive private enterprise tends in general to be more efficient than public ownership and operation. We are also fearful of having so much economic power put in the hands of the state, since we believe that it would inevitably fall into the hands of bureaucrats who have nearly always shown themselves intolerant of human freedom. Had we been in England, we would not have re-nationalized the steel mills.

If one word can be used to describe our philosophy, I would say that we are "distributivists." We do not believe in a concentration of power but rather in its broad distribution. Our goal would be to provide everyone with enough power to be secure against external tyranny but not to permit anyone to have so much power that he could become a tyrant. It will be evident from all this that we agree with Lord Acton's aphorism that absolute power corrupts absolutely.

But as I have hinted, it is not only governments which can have excessive economic power. Private corporations can and some commonly do have excessive power as well. We are especially aware of the evil effects of private monopoly and of highly imperfect competition. Almost invariably this results in a restriction of output below what it would be under pure competition and hence in a reduction of the real national income. This at the same time puts a ceiling on employment and ultimately restricts the investment of capital lest the increased output of industry should lower monopoly prices. We believe therefore that monopoly and quasi-monopoly fosters business instability and helps to make economic recessions and depressions sharper and more pronounced.

Competition and a broader distribution of economic power are therefore a stabilizing force. They are also stabilizing psychologically, since they save business leaders from the dizziness and mistaken judgments which are fostered by the possession of extreme power. The much vaunted claim that bigness promotes discovery and innovation because of its greater ability to support expensive research laboratories has been proved largely erroneous. Most of the fundamental industrial discoveries and innovations have come from smaller firms and plants, as has been well demonstrated by Daniel de Si-

mone of the Department of Commerce and the staff of
Senator Hart's Anti-Monopoly Subcommittee.

The oxygen process and continuous casting, for example, were developed in a relatively small Austrian steel
mill. But the big American companies have been slow
to accept these superior innovations which, although
they require replacement of much of the present plant,
also lower costs and ultimately require less fixed
capital. Businesses often fear innovations. Private research institutions can fall into a rut almost as badly as
governmental bodies. We are just beginning to realize
the innovative benefits of greater competition and a
somewhat smaller scale of plants and companies. We
therefore believe that government should protect the
competitive system as such against the efforts of the big
to crush the smaller and more competitive elements. If
I may give an illustration, I would favor breaking up
U.S. Steel. I would also favor breaking up General Motors into several corporations, based on the similarity of
the automobiles which are produced by the different
divisions.

We believe in the Sherman and Clayton Acts and seek
to defend them against the efforts of big business to sub-
vert and overthrow them. We thus seek to protect the
private enterprise system from the suicidal tendencies
of many of those who most loudly and falsely claim to be
its exponents. For our labor we are commonly denounced
by the false friends of private enterprise who often mud-
dy the waters so thoroughly that those whom we seek to

protect quite frequently become our most savage enemies.

We believe, however, that there is unfair as well as fair competition and that bribing the employees and trying to steal the production secrets of competitors is unethical. Honest competition in goodness of quality and lowness of price are characteristics which should be fostered and not penalized. But this is not to be done by degrading employees, cheating the cities by creating low-tax havens and sanctuaries, or corrupting public officials. If I may close on a minor note, I have just been out to St. Louis, Missouri, and to East St. Louis in my state. I found that one huge company had incorporated a town on the site of its plant, just south of East St. Louis. The town had only 100 citizens but employed, I think, 5,000 people. It escaped paying its share of taxes for educating the children of the employees, escaped paying any welfare costs, escaped supporting police and fire systems (except those needed for internal security), escaped contributing to roads and garbage collection—and threw all those costs on the proverty stricken city of East St. Louis.

There is a similar "town" north of East St. Louis with a somewhat smaller population of 93, where a company had done the same thing. And again, there is a "town" on the Missouri side of the river called Champ, C-h-a-m-p, which has only ten people. And there is the famous case of the many-hundred-million-dollar plant in the Jersey meadows, incorporated into a "town" of 43 people.

Now, this is more common than you think. And what

it means is that the whole burden of local taxation is distorted. That is a minor note to end on. Let me say I wish I could be here when Mr. Powell speaks. I hope he will have a manuscript; he can read mine, and I'll read his, and then we'll join together two weeks from tonight.

SECOND LECTURE

J. ENOCH POWELL

This is one of those questions which have the appearance of being capable of an experimental or objective answer, but which, on examination, prove to refer us back to matters of opinion and intent. It is a debating proposition. It is a proposition in a debate which mankind will never conclude and in which the tides and currents will continue to flow back and forth. Those of us who today offer our own answer to the question are borne on those tides and currents and are indicators of their direction. The question is not so much analogous to "how ought a lunar spaceship to be constructed?" as to "where is human happiness to be found?"

I preface my answer with this warning because the deceptive word "should" in the question could easily be thought to imply some standard or starting point from which the due scope and limits of government can be logically deduced. It is not possible by investigating the nature of man or the characteristics of the human species to discover what form of government is appropriate or "right." The attempt will never be made with more self-confidence or nobility than it was by the draftsmen of your Declaration of Independence. But it was, and is, foredoomed to failure because of its hopeless circularity.

Politically considered—that is, considered under the aspect of government—man is known and is knowable only in actual societies. The idea that these societies are made up of individuals, in the sense of being manufactured from individuals, is mythology, and bad mythology. The individual is self-conscious politically only as a member of a political society. Indeed, this self-consciousness of its members is an inseparable attribute of the existence of a political society, much as individual self-consciousness is an inseparable attribute of individual human existence.

Now, a political society is unthinkable without government. In fact, the statement is tautological; for politics is about government. When we ask questions about the scope of government in a political society, we are making a distinction which is unreal, namely, between government and nongovernment. You cannot, as it were, draw a circle, representing a political society, divide it in two, shade one half, and say; "this is government; the other is not." Of course, for convenience we commonly talk in this way, referring for example, to "the public sector" and "the private sector," expressions which conjure up that very image. But for our purpose tonight this will not serve. For our purpose, government, a common will to be governed, a common self-consciousness of being a political society, is coextensive with that society itself. It is all government.

We can therefore observe, classify, and compare societies, according to their forms of government, but not according to their respective quantums of government. We can also observe those forms changing; and as we do so, we can observe the corresponding change in the self-consciousness or opinion of their members. It is convenient—in fact, it is probably unavoidable—to treat the changes in opinion as the *cause* of the changes in form; and this perhaps does no harm so long as we remember that we are falsifying by separating two aspects of the same phenomenon and identifying them as cause and effect respectively. We ourselves, in our own political character, participate in these changes by holding and expressing opinions, as I am doing in this lecture.

I have not, I am afraid, quite reached the end of my preamble, so anxious am I to emphasize that the differences which we call more or less government—bigger or smaller government, in the terms of the question—are really differences between sorts or methods of government, and between the corresponding opinions about government. If I might put the point in epigrammatic form, the decision not positively to govern is itself a decision of government; or again, sovereignty can be and always is exercised passively as well as actively, but it is still sovereignty. Let me give two examples, writ large across the pages of human history.

Man is a religious animal: he has to form and express opinions about the relationship between himself, his species, and the universe in which it was created or evolved. In many political societies it has seemed during long periods of time to be a "self-evident truth" that all their members must evince the same religious beliefs and participate in the same religious ceremonies; and rewards and punishments, privileges and disadvantages, have been organized and distributed accordingly. At other times the former relationship between what was conceivable and what was inconceivable has been inverted: the community not merely became disinterested in the imposition of religious uniformity but became interested in maintaining one of the several possible alternative systems, that, namely, called religious tolerance. (The other possibilities, which have been, and still are, exemplified, include the sanction of more than one religious conformity—two, for instance, as in Switzerland—or of different conformities in different areas—as in the sixteenth century Holy Roman Empire.) The point I wish to emphasize is that freedom of religious observance is itself a system, in which the political community can be actively interested, using the common instruments of sovereignty —from approval to condign punishment—in order to sustain it. This you acknowledge when you recognize it, as I understand you do, as part of "the American way of life." You are politically intolerant of that uniformity which seemed an essential of a political society in the Massachusetts settlements just as much as it did in Restoration England or as it does in contemporary Spain.

We are accustomed, because of our Western experience, to view the substitution of the one system for the

other as a linear and perhaps irreversible development—
"progress," we are accustomed to say in such cases. It
may therefore be easier to grasp the fact that the approval and enforcement of spontaneous relations between
members of society *is* also government, in an instance
where there has been an alternation or oscillation between
opposite systems in our own historical experience.

Over a wide area of mankind, geographically and
historically, it has been accepted as self-evident that the
economic relations of the members of society should be
determined by rule and conscious authority. That the
economic tasks to be performed by the community could
only be defined and allocated among its members if this
was done by the specific exercise of authority seemed as
obvious as did the necessity of uniform religious observance. How else could a man know what to sow and reap,
any more than how to pray and sacrifice? How else,
indeed, could the society itself survive?

Then, with increasing consciousness, some of the
Western societies began to adopt an alternative system,
namely, that the members of the community should
define and allocate the economic tasks by a system which
dispensed with—indeed, was incompatible with—specific
decisions taken in advance and imposed by authority. It
was the system which has become known under various
names as "laissez-faire" (which implies the opposite thesis
to the one I am sustaining), as "capitalism" (which
places the emphasis on the productive aspect), as "the
market" (which places it on the distributive aspect) or

under more emotive terms, such as "private enterprise" or "the free economy." In this phase, not only was the legal and institutional framework which corresponded to the old system dismantled and demolished but the sovereign power was employed instead to maintain and improve the new system and to police the pattern of relationships between the members of society which now appeared to be as "self-evident" as the one it had superseded. The same rewards and punishments were meted out to sustain the new system as the old—only that what was previously virtuous had become vicious, and vice-versa. What the medieval guild did with approval earned deportation for the Dorsetshire laborers of Tolpuddle and penalties for the duPont Corporation.

It would be a fascinating speculation, into which I cannot now enter, why the substitution of a spontaneous system for a prescribed system in the religious organization of Western societies has presented the appearance of an irreversible movement, while in their economic organization it has undergone, and is still undergoing, a marked reversal. One explanation is possibly that other conformities in behavior and belief have been substituted for religious conformity. At any rate, of the swing of the pendulum in economic organization there is no question. In what were the typical free enterprise countries of the past, on both sides of the Atlantic, men are reverting to the pre-capitalist attitude of mind, which finds it impossible to credit that the economic life of society can continue at all, let alone be satisfactory, unless the tasks and resources are specifically prescribed and allocated by authority. The underlying presumption is altering back again to what it was two centuries and more ago; and the symptom of this change is that more direction is now accepted as the natural remedy for current evils as unhesitatingly as was less direction a hundred years ago. In Britain today more and more people of all classes and parties approach with frank incredulity the working of the price mechanism, even when it is functioning under their own noses and when they use it themselves in their own daily lives. The proposition, for instance, that with free rates of exchange international payments would automatically balance is dismissed as incredible in itself, quite apart from debate upon the merits or otherwise of the method. This is a sign that something stronger than reason is at work.

On the surface, at any rate, the trend appears to owe nothing to the influence of explicitly centralizing or authoritarian theories such as socialism. On the contrary, it is one of history's little ironies that these very same years are witnessing in the European Communist countries an enthusiastic and excited re-discovery and exploration of the market method of establishing economic tasks and allocating resources. This has already led in some of these countries, notably in Hungary, to the establishment of classically perfect models of the way a market system works. This strange sort of epicycle on the wave movement of history is more than a matter for ironic amusement. It is a useful reminder of the fact,

which I have stressed already, that adoption and maintenance of the market system for regulating the economic behavior of citizens is itself an aspect of government.
We in the West are accustomed to associate the market
system with the ideas of personal liberty, freedom of the
individual, and so forth; historically we see it as part of
the nineteenth century liberal creed. Yet its adoption
in Eastern Europe owes nothing to such associations or
theories, and is not felt to be inconsistent with the ethos
and outlook of a Communist state. Whether the working
of the market system will not itself produce other social
and psychological changes inconsistent with a Communist regime, is a different question, and remains to be
seen.

The case of Eastern Europe, however, brings me con-
veniently to the ground on which it seems to me debate
can most rationally be conducted about the limits or
size not of government—we have, I hope, refined our
definition beyond that point—but of government by
specific prescription as opposed to government by the
maintenance of a spontaneous or automatic system of
decision. Now, the opposite to specific is undefined.
(Both terms are, of course, used a priori, from the point
of view of someone looking forward; for in hindsight,
a posteriori, all events—the outcome of all decisions,
however reached and implemented—are equally specific.) The key distinction is between a method on the
one hand which presumes a specific object, defined in
advance, and a method on the other hand which dispenses

with such an object, or with any object at all that cannot be stated in the most general terms.

With this distinction in mind we are in a position to analyze the application of government to the different areas into which the life of a political society can be divided, beginning naturally with its relations with other political societies—nations, for short. In all these relationships, whether peaceable or violent, it sees itself and behaves as a unit, as an individual entering into relationship with other individuals. An individual, however, if he entertains an intention at all, can only entertain a specific intention. For this reason it is unthinkable that a nation should have several inconsistent foreign or defense policies at the same time, or that it should be content to discover after the event what its defense or foreign policy has been. External policy, whether of the State Department or Pentagon variety, is inherently unitary and therefore inherently specific. It must be decided once for all the society's members, and that decision must be enforced upon them all, for instance, by the levying of taxation which a deliberate decision applies to the construction and manning of carrier task forces or squadrons of F-111 aircraft.

Turning inwards, we encounter first the administration and enforcement of law, the framework without which the society itself, of whatever type it may be, is unthinkable. The nature of law is to be specific, and to include its administration and enforcement in the sphere of specific government is little more than a tautology.

Yet it is worth pausing a moment on these last two examples to observe how a specific intention is frequently also limited and thus arbitrary.

The general object of defense policy is the national security, which is an absolute and total object. Yet the policy itself is limited arbitrarily to a certain quantum of defensive preparations. In Britain we have made a fetish of a defense budget representing 6 percent of an assumed national income, or £2,000 million "at 1964 prices." You in the United States have opted for ABMs against China but not against Russia. There is always a stopping point; and that, like the content of the preparations themselves, is decided unitarily and therefore, in the most literal sense of the word, "arbitrarily"—a derivative from *arbitrium,* individual judgment.

Likewise the object of administration and enforcement of the law is absolute, that it shall never be infringed. Yet the specific intention—to maintain such and such a judiciary, and to recruit and equip such and such a police force—is limited and arbitrary: the line is drawn somewhere by a common decision. Out beyond that line some of the functions, particularly the preventive rather than the punitive, are discharged by a different process of decision. We in Britain have seen in recent years the growth of a whole private enterprise industry engaged in protecting citizens' property—performing in other words, part of the indisputably public function of watch and ward. The numbers of guard dogs and nightwatchmen, not to say armored vans and escorts for cashiers, are determined by one process, the numbers of policemen by another; yet it is impossible to draw any valid dividing line between their functions: they overlap. It is a case not uninstructive and one with large applications in other spheres, to which we shall come later.

There is probably no society in which the scope of common intentions and therefore of specific government has been strictly limited to its external relations and the internal administration of law, which may be regarded as the theoretical absolute minimum. The consciousness of identity and unity spills over, often far beyond, and can result in specific intentions being formed and enforced over a wide area of the citizens' lives. If I might start with an example close to the boundary line of the minimum, the United States government has decreed huge and continuing expenditures upon space research and astronautics, which may be in part, but must be far from wholly, motivated by considerations of defense. Whence the rest? Why does a government decide, like Pharaoh commanding the erection of a pyramid, that large slabs of the energy of its citizens shall be devoted to the specific end of putting a man on the moon or a probe on Venus? Because (if I may be allowed to personify for a moment) the nation is thinking unitarily, self-consciously, analogously to its self-consciousness in ordinary external affairs. It is thinking like you and me when we decide to go in for a bridge or a golf championship. The government is acting on an impulse akin to that of emulation in the individual, and is able to enforce its specific decisions and the sacrifices (less emotively, the opportunity costs) which they involve, because that sense of emulation is felt by the citizenry at large and attached by them to the national totem. "If we are first to put a man on the moon," says the nation, as it were with one voice, "it will be a feather in our collective cap, and we shall all be pleased and proud of ourselves. Therefore we must all club together and build a capsule." While this example of a prestige activity—the word had to come at last!—is modern, there is nothing new about the thing. Basically the United States is not acting differently from the German princeling of the eighteenth century who charged his subjects for a magnificent opera house or the council of the Greek city-states which reared those wonderful pediments and columns at Paestum and Agrigentum.

It is not accidental that the more a nation approaches the totalitarian model—that is, the wider the area of its life covered by specific government—the more marked becomes the feature of international emulation. In every department, from agriculture to sport—yes, sport above all!—the way has to be found to whip up the spirit of emulation and put the nation in a competitive context or "league table" beside other nations. It is the mood appropriate to specific government; and the wider specific government extends, the more it requires and stimulates that mood for its own maintenance. We shall meet it again when we come to "growth"; but the thought is worth bearing in mind, meanwhile, as we look at the areas covered by the welfare state in the widest and loosest application of that term.

When the United States decided to put a man on the moon as soon as possible, it was setting on one side the specific results proposed from devoting resources to this object and on the other side the bundle of unknown and unknowable results which would have accrued if those resources had not been earmarked by the government at all; and it decided that it not only did not know what the latter were but that it did not care and was not going to find out, because it had made up its mind to plump for Apollo. In other words, it was treating the lunar result as *incommensurable* with the alternatives. This is the true hallmark of specific, centralized decision: it treats all magnitudes as incommensurables. That is the reason why those who protest against such decisions always oppose to them others of the same kind. For instance, in Britain the nuclear disarmers and their kidney are always translating expenditure of Polaris or the like into expenditure on other public projects. They say: "this weapon is equivalent to so-and-so many new hospitals in the National Health Service." (In fact, we almost use the hospital as a unit of measurement in our defense debates.) They do not say: "If we did not have this weapon, we should all be better off in all kinds of ways which cannot be predicted but which would be jolly nice." It is easier to stick to incommensurables, and try to knock one down with another.

This is basically what happens in all specific government decisions on consumption, especially on consumption of services, such as education and medicare. The collective voice is saying: "We do not know what the alternatives are and we wish for no rational comparison with them, because 'secondary education for all,' or 'free medical attention,' or 'a guaranteed minimum income for all' are GOOD THINGS, and we are going to have them or arrange to believe that we have them, whatever else." All this sort of "good things," which I have capitalized, are incommensurable with one another and with the other kinds of good thing about which no one would dream of talking in the same way. No one says: "A family car is a good thing and I will have it without considering if I could instead have, for the same or less effort, a trip to Europe, a nicer apartment, or a technical qualification for my daughter."

The inclusion of education amongst those last alternatives is a reminder that there is nothing objective about a good or a service which puts it among the incommensurables for any particular society, but the opinion held in that society, which of course can and does change with the passage of time. If there were a nation of coal worshippers—perhaps in some unexplored part of Latin America there is!—it might well appear to them a good thing that 200 million tons of coal a year should be excavated and ceremonially burnt; specific decisions of government would be taken to secure that result; and it would appear to the citizen to be perfectly irrelevant whether more energy and more of the desirable things which energy affords could be obtained with less effort in other ways. Along this subjective line runs the boundary between the welfare state and the state-planned economy.

As with other specific decisions of government, those directed to securing the consumption of certain goods and services which characterize the welfare state are in appearance absolute but in reality arbitrary and limited. The apparent universals "secondary education for all" or "medicare for all" conceal decisions on what "secondary education" and "medicare" are and how much of them is to be provided. The British National Health Service is an institution which enshrines the decision that medical care in Great Britain shall be of a certain amount, quality, and composition—no less and no more—no better and no worse. It is optional whether an addition, unforeseeable and unspecified by the community, is permitted to be made to that total by methods of spontaneous decision. We are today debating in Britain whether such an addition to the quantum of school education shall be prevented or forbidden, much as if it were made unlawful to supplement the police with watchmen and burglar alarms.

As, again, with other specific decisions of government, there is a strong element of national self-consciousness, both inward-looking and outward-looking, in the specific decisions characteristic of the welfare state. The very expression "welfare state" emphasizes the unitary nature of the decisions to allocate resources in a specific way, and these decisions are commended by emotive expressions—"the Great Society," "the compassionate society," and so on—which appeal to solidarity. Externally, the nationalistic motive has long been in evidence. The assertion that the British National Health Service is the envy and admiration of the world has been repeated since 1948 with a fervor which betrays the force of motivation. Years before that, rivalry with Germany was urged over and over in the early development in Britain of the state education and social insurance systems; and more recently in debates on the expansion of technical and university education, "league tables" have been brandished similar to those that feature in debates in the economic field, to which I now at last come.

All actions, from whatever motive taken, are attended by economic consequences. Whether men build a cathedral or a battleship or a hospital or a factory, the total disposition of effort and resources throughout the country as a result is different from what it would have been if they had not taken that decision. In this sense, all decisions are economic decisions. There is, however, another and more useful sense of the term, in which I intend hereafter to use it. If you will revert to my imaginary nation of coal worshippers, you will recall that, but for their propensity to worship coal, they would have treated it like any other source of energy, and would have compared the advantage and disadvantage of digging it with the advantages and disadvantages of all the alternative ways in which their energies might be employed. In order to make such a comparison, one must have a common scale, and I doubt not that they would have been sufficiently advanced in civilization to have used money for this purpose. It was their attitude of mind towards coal which prevented them from doing this, and so rendered coal incommensurable—for them—with other things. It turned something which for us is (I hope) an economic decision (how much coal, if any, to excavate) into a noneconomic decision. An economic decision therefore is the result of a choice between alternatives which are regarded as commensurable in terms of a common scale, namely, money.

Note, by the way, that in practice money renders commensurable even things which are themselves not directly priced. For example, if I prefer teaching a class at £20 a week to driving a bulldozer at £40 a week, I am using money to compare the personal satisfactions I anticipate from the two occupations, even though nobody could price them directly, since anyhow, being my own, they are unique.

What happens when government is said to plan or control the economy, in whole or in part—when government takes economic decisions—is that it extends specificity to the choice between commensurables. In circumstances where, by common consent, the rightness or wrongness of a decision is judged by its superiority to all others as measured in monetary terms, the government itself takes one out of all the possible decisions and uses the resources of sovereignty to put that decision into effect. Expressed in another way, it chooses in advance one specific pattern of economic activity as being foreseeably "right," that is, better than all possible alternatives, and sets itself to realize that pattern.

Those who advocate introducing or maintaining this system for defining economic tasks and allocating resources between them, as opposed to the alternative system of permitting the tasks to be defined and the resources allocated through comparisons made in money terms by means of the market, must really be making one of two assertions.

Quite often, they are asserting that the specific decisions taken by government are *inherently* superior to all alternatives; that is, they are transplanting the boundary line between economic and noneconomic decisions, so as to include government decisions among the noneconomic. Much "growthmanship" is of this kind. The nationalist motive of emulation is plain in the frequent assertion that an economy must be made to "grow" at so much percent per annum because the nation is being left behind by other nations in the league tables of growth. This proposition is no more or less rational than the decision to be first, if possible, to put a man on the moon. It is equally noneconomic, because it excludes courses of action—such as an increase in leisure or in activities not statistically measured—which might have given greater total satisfaction if treated as commensurable with "growth." It also illustrates admirably the unavoidable specificity of all such government decisions, because a growth target can only be realized through deliberate action if it is expressed as a defined and unique bundle of goods and services to be produced and consumed during a future period of time.

The alternative assertion is to maintain that government is able to predict not merely the results which the market would have thrown up—if that were all, there would be no point in bothering—but the results which it would have thrown up if it had been a theoretically perfect, or at least a less imperfect, measuring instrument. We have a story in Britain about the Duke of Wellington who, when accosted by a stranger with the words "Mr. Smith, I believe," replied: "If you believe that, Sir, you'll believe anything." The predictions of governments have so regularly been in error on the largest and broadest of assessments—error which has been revealed by the market itself and which governments have eventually been obliged to admit—that it requires a credulity even greater than that of the Duke of Wellington's stranger to suppose that governments are superior instruments of economic judgment.

What is experimentally demonstrated about the economic predictions of government can be accounted for in theory; for governments suffer from the twin defects of paucity of information and debility of motive. It is inherent in specific government decisions of an economic nature that they are unitary and therefore centralized, and also that they are premature. Both characteristics automatically exclude an enormous mass of information which the market is capable of digesting. The market works continuously and receives impressions from any and every source: the processes of exploration, investigation, and decision are not separated but coincide. This is something which no system involving a centralized and conscious judgment can rival. For the same reason the market does not have to produce decisions too soon: prematurity is one of the great but unavoidable sources of error in conscious deliberation. The market does not have to decide in advance whether natural gas will be found in the North Sea, nor how much, nor what it will cost to exploit it. A National Economic Plan for 1970 has to decide all these things in advance; yet there is no means whereby, except accidentally, it can know them in advance. Add to all this that the economic decisions of government, being public and political, are subject to the pressures of opinion and that it is preferable in the short run to defer to that opinion rather than to be guided by the logical implications of the information available. Even if a government knew that half the coal mines would close in the following decade, it would be virtually impossible for it to take overt decisions to that effect.

In order to admit that specific decision of government is immensely inferior to the market as an instrument of economic judgment, it is not necessary to assert that the market system is perfect or capable of being rendered so. Quite apart from the plausible argument that a degree of imperfection is inherent in the market—that is, that with theoretically complete information everywhere the market could not work at all—the natural inference is that the activity of government ought to be directed to minimizing the avoidable imperfections, as by anti-monopoly and anti-restrictive practice legislation and policing. And here I conclude by observing once again that a free market system, properly understood, is itself a form of government, a method of regulating the economic relations between citizens which is enormously superior in efficiency to the alternative—provided always that the common object is itself economic.

REBUTTALS

J. ENOCH POWELL

A most annoying thing has happened. There is evidently
an individual bearing the same name as myself, who has
been going about the United States, expressing all sorts
of opinions which of course he is perfectly entitled to
hold but which I happen not to share and some of which
I abominate. As ill luck would have it, Mr. Douglas has
come across this individual and—quite pardonably—
mistaken him for me. The consequence has been that Mr.
Douglas and I have largely missed one another in the
dark.

I must say however that if I happen to catch up with
this tiresome namesake of mine, I shall give him a piece
of my mind: in many instances I am wholly in agreement with the criticism Mr. Douglas levels at him. For
example, this gentleman, if such he be, is—I quote from
the Senator—"touring the country to expound his opposition to subsidies"; but apparently he wants the postal
services to be subsidized both internally—by cross-subsi-
dization—and externally—at the expense of the taxpayer. I don't: I regard the post office at home as a
service which ought to pass an economic criterion. I

therefore not only don't want it subsidized. I want it denationalized—mail, telephones, and all. I share too in Britain the hostility which the Senator expresses to the public subsidizing of shipbuilding, shipping, and air transport (where I am also a denationalizer).

Moreover this Powell-fellow is obviously a "blimp," as we say, of the very worst description: he—and I quote again the Senator's words—"pleads for the restoration of the British Empire in the days of Lord Salisbury," while my own object has long been to help my countrymen to realize that that Empire has not only gone forever but never did exist, outside their own heated imaginations, in the imperialistic sense attributed to it during the present century. And what the other man means by "claiming that it is the worship of the British King (whomever that individual may be) which enabled the flag to go to the Rocky Mountains," I can't imagine. Like the Senator, I too had always assumed this was due to "the initiative of the American frontiersmen."

All this is a thousand pities, because there is so much, and so much of importance, about which the Senator and I warmly agree. While I don't share his antipathy to jet air travel—a harmless foible, surely, and I hope I never have any foibles worse than that—he too emphasized the point which I was concerned to labor in my own paper, namely, that private enterprise and competition don't just happen—nor, if they do happen, do they just go on happening. Private enterprise and competition are themselves a system, not to say a way of life, and as such they must be maintained and policed and, as far as possible, deliberately perfected. Whether or not the Senator would share my philosophy in classifying them as a form of government, he would repudiate as I do the dangerous implication of that phrase, laissez-faire, that the free enterprise system is something you can leave and walk away. It is not. Its preservation is a proper, indeed an essential, field for government action. In this connection he brings out an important additional point, that as the market process is essentially an investigation process, for obtaining and utilizing information, government is properly concerned not only with preventing and punishing the deliberate conveyance of false information but with enforcing the maximum disclosure of true information. We have in this respect been making progress in Britain, though probably not yet enough, in the reform of our company law.

Other major propositions in which the Senator's heart and mine beat as one are his plea for the decentralization of power, his reminder that there is no correlation between the bigness of an undertaking and its efficiency, still less its propensity to innovate, and his insistence on the preservation of the individual's scope for choice, even for choice of privacy. None of these propositions is self-fulfilling: there has to be a deliberate and determined action by the community as a whole to give effect to them. It is a common but pernicious error to confuse specific action by the state to preserve the right of choice for individuals with specific action by the state to make choices on behalf of individuals. These are not cognate activities; they are contrary activities, and where economic ends are acknowledged as the criterion, there is nothing to compare with the working of the market, price, and profit, as a guarantee of the decentralization of power, of the optimum size of undertakings, and of the individual's opportunity to choose. The market decentralizes power right down to every individual consumer, so that a grand, continuous general election is in progress the whole time, a vote being cast whenever a share or a security or an article or a service is bought and sold. This is an economic democracy in which there are no privileges—everybody's dollar is as good as everybody else's dollar—and one where the mightiest of corporations and capitalists have had to bow to the collective wishes of the humblest citizens. In the economic sphere one might regard the regulative activity of the state as a kind of civic rights guarantee.

Finally, I was much struck by the fact that the Senator and I made the same diagnosis of the motivation of many forms of specific government, namely that they are expressions of a collective self-consciousness, where the community, personified by its members and acting like a person, obeys emotional stimuli such as envy or emulation; and curiously, he and I both happened upon the space program to illustrate and typify the point.

All this being so, I feel I can most usefully contribute to this stage of our debate by putting my point of view on three major subjects thrown up by the Senator's lecture and the discussion which immediately followed it. The first is that with which a great part of the discussion was preoccupied, namely this: granted that the community settles upon a common object, e.g., the provision of education, and consequently employs specific government—direct public action—to attain it, how is the quantity to be limited and defined? Education and medical care, for instance, are not absolutes: both in quantity and in quality an infinite spectrum exists, while for practical purposes potential demand is unlimited. There is no finite, objective "need" for such and such education, such and such medical care, so that, having "met" that "need," we can walk away and get on with something else. Where the market operates in the economic sphere, limits set themselves spontaneously by the jostling of one demand against another in the effort to become "effective"; but where a single, public decision is taken, the market is *ipso facto* cut out and there is no alternative criterion which will tell us that X percent of the national income or Y billion dollars is the "right" amount of public education or of medicare.

What in practice happens is that a sort of pseudo-market is established at the political level: the vote-pulling potentials of more education and more medicare jostle with one another and with the vote-losing potential of more taxation (including the modern refinement of taxation known as inflation). Presumably this is what we intended when we made these decisions political, for we must be presumed, even though the presumption be somewhat over-charitable, to have intended the natural consequences of our actions. It can happen however that, so crude are the political decisions taken necessarily once on behalf of all, that they differ widely from the quantity or quality which would have given maximum satisfaction to the citizens. They might, for instance, have preferred less spent on education and more on health or vice versa. I used myself, when Minister of Health, to aver that in the absence of the National Health Service more medical care, rather than less, would probably have got itself provided. Certainly more hospitals would have been built in postwar Britain, and built sooner. This leads me to the only practical advice I can offer on the controversy which raged during the discussion with Senator Douglas—namely, that wherever the good or service is such that it could alternatively have been chosen and defined by market processes, particular care should be taken to keep the market alternative in existence, and great vigilance should be exercised to detect, and respond to, evidence that the common objective could be satisfied by the spontaneous choices of the citizens. Where, alas, as with our National Health Service, the public service is by definition both universal and free to the consumer, I am afraid that those precepts have become counsels of perfection.

The second subject raised, if only in passing, by the Senator's paper, to which I should like to devote a few minutes, is that of minimum wage legislation. I cannot, of course, discuss this in its application to specifically

American conditions. I have already been too long in the United States, a matter of ten days, to suppose that I know all about your affairs. But in general it illustrates the way in which the same, noneconomic object can be achieved either in ways which interfere directly with the working of the market or which do so as little as possible. Let me take it that the noneconomic object here is to secure a certain minimum standard of living for all members of the community. I call it noneconomic in the sense that if a voice from heaven were to tell us that by doing so we would all be worse off as a result, we would reply "Go to ——, go to ——, that is not what we are interested in, we are pursuing other objects."

Now, if this minimum standard of living is the object, then the attempt to fix a minimum price for labor appears to me a disastrously clumsy means to the end. If price is fixed at a higher level than it would be in the open market—and this must be the presumed effect of legislative prescription—the automatic and unavoidable consequence is that demand is reduced. In this case, insofar as the legislation is effective, it must reduce the demand for labor; in other words, cause—or increase—unemployment. There is no way in which this can be avoided except by enforcing the employment of the same quantity of labor as before; but then in that event everything else in the economy would have to be forcibly adjusted, so as to fit.

In addition to all this, the measure is also ineffective redistributively, in that it operates alike upon the income of large families and small, of families with exceptional handicaps and of families with none. Surely measures directed towards specific circumstances and working by deliberate redistribution—such as family allowances—would be more efficient and would distort the allocation of effort and resources through the market less.

The last point I wish to raise is the exception to the general principle of maximizing competition—a principle on which I think we both agree—which the Senator appears to admit but which I do not: namely, combination to fix the price of labor through unions at a higher price than it would have commanded in the open market. Actually, I happen to believe that the net effect of trade unions is to lower, not raise, the price of labor, by deforming the market; but the objections seem to me the same even if unions did in the long run raise the price of their members' labor.

In talking about unions, we are not talking about voluntary associations, men availing themselves of the basic human freedom of free association, We are talking about groups endowed by legislation with immunity from civil or criminal responsibility which would otherwise attach to the actions which they contemplate. These actions consist in forcing the seller or buyer of labor—for, of course, I include employers' unions as well as employees' unions—to fix a different price from that otherwise payable, by means of coercion brought upon one citizen, or one set of citizens, by their fellows. In this sense all trade union action is restrictive—because it depends for its effect on depriving citizens of the freedom to make lawful bargains or to perform lawful acts, as they otherwise would wish to do. I do not believe that any tenable justification, either moral or economic, has ever been advanced for this type of legislation, and I am surprised to find the Senator defending it. He does so on the ground, frequently advanced, of the supposed weakness of the bargaining position of the workman, who must dispose of his labor currently while the purchaser, so the argument runs, can wait. Again, I happen to believe that this ground itself is fallacious—for one reason, among many, that if valid at all it applies not only to those who sell labor but to those who, for instance, sell strawberries, professional advice, or electricity. However, supposing that it were valid, and that a factor of X ought to be added to the bargaining power, i.e., to the price, of labor, then surely two things would follow. First, we ought to prohibit employers' unions, since the object is *ex hypothesi* to increase the bargaining power of the sellers of labor. To use the same methods to increase the bargaining power of the buyers of labor must surely defeat the purpose in general. Secondly, the process must surely be applied universally, by the regulative power of the community, and not left to the haphazard and catch-as-catch-can effect of private privileged combination here or there. In short, it ought to take the form not merely of minimum wage regulation but of the regulation of all wages and salaries so that they stand at a higher level than that which would be fixed in the market. But we have already seen that this is both absurd and harmful—which only shows what difficulties and inefficiencies we incur when we seek to achieve our objects either by destroying competition or by resorting to specific government regulation of economic effort.

PAUL H. DOUGLAS

I am glad to join in welcoming Mr. and Mrs. Powell to this country and to express the hope that they may find their visit both pleasant and fruitful.

I think there probably are two Powells, but not two Powells traveling in the United States at the same time. Rather there is one Powell, a very leading member of the Conservative or Tory party in Great Britain, and another Powell now appearing here before an American audience.

Now, I had to prepare my paper last week, before Mr. Powell came, but I was given from the Congressional Library a very good volume of his speeches entitled *A Nation Not Afraid*, so I based what I had to say about him on these speeches delivered in England which he may, apparently, not quite agree with as the Powell who is traveling in this country.

I have great respect for Mr. Powell, although I do not share his mystical attachment to the British monarchy as evidenced in the last speech of his in this book, delivered before the St. George Society in England. In it, I suppose very pardonably, he was carried away by the exuberance of his own verbosity and claimed for the British monarchy the inspiration which caused Englishmen to get out to the Rocky Mountains, which I had always thought John C. Fremont and Jim Bridger had attained. I respect Mr. Powell as a man with independence of mind and political courage. To have twice resigned from a position of leadership in the Tory party because it was not sufficiently orthodox in its financial policies and not sufficiently cognizant of the abilities of R. A. Butler, Reginald Maulding, Iain MacLeod and certain other members, stamps him as a man of decision and not a pale habitué of the Cliveden set, either of the old or modern style.

Peeping through the foliage of his philosophical rhetoric as expressed in his paper of last week, moreover, there are hints of Mr. Powell's distrust of the international race to put a man on the moon, which I am very glad to have him reaffirm now, and which I am proud to have voted against because it was consuming nearly $3.5 billion a year and will cost in all at least $20 billion. I expected him, therefore, to be similarly allergic to proposals to spend billions on the supersonic airliner to enable the jet sets of our two countries to save a few hours of time in the air, which they will probably then misspend on land. I am distressed that apparently he does not join me in opposing this supersonic airliner.

There are many other forms of wasteful expenditure upon which I think we could intellectually agree. But in dealing with these, I had the advantage in the

United States Senate of being able to express my convictions on roll calls and to bear the opposition of the subsidized businesses of this country which, on paper, seem to have the same philosophy as Mr. Powell, while the teller system of the House of Commons made it almost impossible for him to assume individual responsibility—it was not his fault—and almost forced him to follow the herd instinct, to follow his fellow Tories down the path of many governmental and business extravagances. I pardon him for this, however, because he was really a captive of the British party system.

I hope our friend will excuse me, however, if I must frankly say that I find his address of last week—and I hope you will forgive me, Mr. Powell, for this—to be singularly weak, ambiguous, and unconvincing. He did much better tonight. But last week was not too good.

MR. POWELL: I had the value of your paper, sir.

SENATOR DOUGLAS: It was not easy for me to follow him through the semantic underbrush by which he sought to make all decisions, whether public or private, political decisions and in which he introduced a distinct note of philosophical relativism by saying that judgments depended on values, the correctness of which could not be measured or tested. I was therefore disappointed in my hope that he might take up the concrete examples of budgetary expenditures which I thought were justified and those which I thought were not, and engage me in battle either on those items or the corresponding expenditures in the budget of his own country. That would have brought the discussion of whether government was too big down out of the clouds into the meaty details of everyday life.

But it was not to be. Our friend retreated instead into the misty cavern of philosophical abstraction, appropriate perhaps for an English don who regards language as a device to conceal thought, but not as the plain, blunt, political engineer which I had thought Enoch Powell to be and which I still persist in believing is the real self beneath all his bland incomprehensibility.

There is, however, one strong thread of argument which Mr. Powell brought out towards the end of his discourse and which he expanded tonight. That is his faith in the superiority of the so-called market to government fiat in the determination of prices and the allocation of energy. It is hard to tell whether this is a remark thrown out over his shoulder to his foes of the Labor party in Albion beyond the seas, or a polite staking out of a suppositious battle ground with what he mistakenly presumes to be the position of the northern branch of the Democratic party in this country, which he correctly senses to be the opponent of the monarchical, aristocratic, and hieratic principle in American political and social life.

I must confess, however, that judging by his discourse of last week, Mr. Powell—and he did much better tonight—does not fully understand the positive merits of "free competitive markets" nor the weaknesses and lim-

itations which should prevent them from being the sole
and at times even the proper predominant measuring
stick. In short, he does not make as strong a case for
competitive markets as he should and at the same time
he is blind to their obvious weaknesses.

Since we should be interested in developing truth
rather than merely trying to win a debating victory, I
feel it only proper to take up the theories which Mr.
Powell has unfortunately allowed to fall from his hand
and to state what I believe to be the positive advantages
of using competitive market price as a guide for many
decisions. I want to make a stronger case for them than
he chose to do.

Within the budget of any individual, market price
furnishes the measuring rod which will enable a man to
get the greatest amount of satisfaction, granted his income. He will do this by apportioning his expenditures
so that the last dollar, or in the case of a Scotsman the
last sixpence, spent on each of the various commodities
and services will yield approximately equal satisfaction.
If this is not the case and the last dollar or the Scot's last
sixpence spent on A yields more satisfaction than the
last dollar or sixpence on B, there will be a transfer of
purchasing power from B to A until there is equality at
the margin. These principles of the diminishing utility
generally provided by successive units of money income
and the resulting equivalence of utility at the margins of
expenditure for an individual give us a measuring system
which governs the apportionment of money by the in-

dividual. In normal times this is far superior to rationing. The same thing, of course, holds true within a business enterprise, where price or marginal revenue determines the point to which production will be carried and enables a system of accounting to exist within the enterprise.

Similarly, amongst professional workers—though I do not think amongst manual workers—a comparison of the pleasures gained from the income derived from the last unit of time spent in work compared with the pain experienced or the other pleasures of leisure foregone, helps to govern the apportionment of time not only within the year but also the life span.

Now I'm going to say something that may sound egotistical, and I hope you will forgive me. Perhaps I may be pardoned, as one who was an early worker in the theory and measurement of production, in pointing out that the equation

$$P = b \, L^K C^{1-K}$$

or, in its better form,

$$P = b \, L^K C^J$$

roughly measures the shares which each factor of production contributes to the total physical or value output. Interestingly enough, there has seemed to be a certain rough rule that an increase of 1 percent in the quantity of labor is associated with an increase of 65 hundredths of 1 percent in product, while an increase of 1 percent in capital seems to be attended with an increase of approximately 35 hundredths of 1 percent in product. Interestingly enough these ratios also seem to be not far from the actual shares received by labor and capital in those economies which have good enough statistics to measure.

In short, I am surprised that Mr. Powell did not develop these and other arguments and, out of a desire to be gallant to our visitor from beyond the seas, I present him with certain reprints which if he studies them will enable him to strengthen his case. I present him not only with a brief brochure that I wrote—but also with a volume, *The Theory and Empirical Analysis of Production,* which has just come out. It costs $12.50—in our money, or that would be almost——

MR. POWELL: Five pounds.

SENATOR DOUGLAS:—five pounds. Almost five pounds in your money. I present this to you and ask that you give it to the library of the Conservative party.

MR. POWELL: Senator, may I be permitted on my return home to send you books or periodicals to a similar value?

SENATOR DOUGLAS: Very good.

I think therefore I understand the degree of truth behind the passionately-held but dimly-defended faith of Mr. Powell. But I think I also understand its weaknesses and I can therefore cast an impartial and appraising eye upon market price as an institution. It is this which prevents me from following the example of Mr. Powell and of some American economists, who shall be nameless, and from bowing like a denizen of the forest before the wooden and blackened image of a pagan diety.

For the plain truth of the matter is that while the

present price system helps an individual to distribute his money and time with relative efficiency, if we take the world as it is, it is very defective when we come to society as a whole with all its inequalities and injustices. The worshippers of market price are fond of saying— and I was glad to hear Mr. Powell say it, because it bore out what I thought he was going to say—that it represents true democracy—that everyone votes but votes from the heart and the brain with dollars rather than with ballots. I was greatly interested to hear Mr. Powell say "Everybody's dollar is as good as anybody else's dollar." That is true. But what he omits and what the apologists omit—and it is a vital omission—is that some vote with millions of dollars and others with but a few scanty hundreds or thousands. And that is the nub of the case. This makes the relative satisfactions as between individuals incommensurable for income as received and for income as spent. I do not wish to dwell unduly on these differences as between individuals lest I be accused of demagogy—a charge which is always leveled if one has struck home. But I ask in all sobriety whether we can say that the last dollar spent by a Tommy Manville or a Barbara Hutton was equal in giving satisfaction or meeting need to that received by a widow striving desperately to feed, clothe, and shelter her brood of fatherless children. It is the patent paradox of wanton luxury existing side by side with deprived poverty which has excited the indignation of so many generous spirits. This indignation has brought down upon the heads of those who hold it the scornful ire of so many British Tories. And yet despite this anger and ridicule, the consciences of both the British and American people have been partially aroused.

There is an increasing resolve not to be quiescent on the subject of poverty but to seek constructively to reduce it.

The plain truth of the matter is that even in our prosperous country nearly one-sixth of the population or over 30 million people are in poverty, while another 16 million are on the fringes of poverty. (And I can only say that if you question the poverty standard I am using —a family of four trying to live on 70 cents a day per person for food and $1.40 a day for all other items, or approximately $3,200 or $3,300 a year—I will defy anyone to try to live on it.) The poor and the near poor therefore number approximately 50 million people. They are not the half of the nation of Jacob Reis, nor the one-third of Franklin Roosevelt's second inaugural, but they are the long-suffering and badly neglected quarter. Or, if you wish to be precise, the badly neglected sixth.

And may I point out that the poorest one-tenth of the population received only 1 percent of the nation's income and that the poorest one-fifth, including of course the poorest tenth, received but 4 percent. At the other extreme, the one-tenth which is best off received somewhere between 27 and 30 percent of the total personal income and the upper one-fifth no less than 41 percent to 43 percent. If you take the surplus income,

namely the dollars of income above the minimum standard of life, you will find of course that the bottom two-
fifths have virtually no surplus and the upper tenth or
the upper fifth have the overwhelming portion of the
surplus. I personally do not believe that such disparities
can be brushed aside.

I submit that if we have any concern for human
values, we cannot take the market demands of the poor
as an adequate measure of their basic human needs. For
this group has very little market demand since it has
very little income. Without advocating equality of income, which I do not, some marked reduction in this
disparity is called for. But it will not be obtained by
market decisions which must take the existing distribution of income for granted. This disparity will not be
greatly reduced by private philanthropy, excellent as
that may be and is. It can only be appreciably reduced
through government policies of taxation and expenditure. On the former side, in my judgment, the rate
should increase rather than decrease as income increases.

On the whole in this country, state and local taxation,
with its emphasis on sales taxes and the general property
tax, is regressive—the percentage paid diminishing as the
income increases. The federal tax system on the other
hand is progressive but because of tax loopholes and
avoidances and evasions it is far less than the published
rates would lead one to believe. I pointed out two weeks
ago that people in the upper income group who, according to the schedules, would be expected to pay 90 per-

cent of their income actually paid an effective average rate of something less than 25 percent, according to figures of a few years ago. Yet the Conservative party in Great Britain, like the conservative coalition in this country, has commonly opposed the principle of progression and has not sought to lessen the market advantages of the rich.

My real trouble with Mr. Powell is not with him as an individual. He is a charming man. I have had the pleasure of meeting with him at dinner, and with his wife. They are charming and very fine. I think he is an estimable man, but unfortunately he is tied up with the Conservative party and has to embrace its principles. And when the votes are called in the House of Commons, he has to follow after them. What is the phrase of Gilbert and Sullivan?

> When in that House MP's divide,
> If they've a brain and cerebellum too,
> They have to leave that brain outside
> And vote just as their leaders tell them to.
> [Laughter.]
> But then the prospect of a lot of statesmen
> All in close proximity
> Thinking for themselves is what no man
> can face with equanimity.
> [Laughter.]

At the spending end of the spectrum, we maintain that the government rather than private industry is the better agency to create a demand for education amongst those who otherwise would not have the funds to pay for it, as for public health measures and recreation—no man can provide Central Park in his own backyard—and a myriad of other purposes which the fiscal conservatives of other years bitterly opposed but which the more enlightened conservatives of today such as Mr. Powell, at least the Mr. Powell who is traveling in this country, now accept. But in America current proposals over the war, or perhaps I should say the skirmish, on poverty are opposed as vehemently as of old. The specific issues may change but the spirit of opposition largely remains the same.

I am afraid that the real reason for conservative opposition to social reform was revealed by Mr. Powell's reply to Mr. Coan's question when the latter in discussion last week asked if human values rather than sheer money demand should not be a guide for social action. You will remember that Mr. Powell twice tossed this query aside by his sharp counter-query of "whose values." Now, forgive me, Mr. Powell, if I say this. I suppose that Pontius Pilate thought he had made a sharp reply when he asked, according to the Gospel as given by John, "What is truth." But neither the Roman procurator nor the British parliamentarian would stay for an answer. If pressed, I suppose the answer would be that the final psychic values of the rich and powerful are as sharp and compelling as those of the poor and miserable. But to maintain this successfully one would have to make the rich and powerful an entirely different and superior race from the poor, so that their pleasure scale would always be at such a higher level than that of the poor that their millionth dollar would yield as much satisfaction as the thousandth dollar of the poor. There was an Englishman by the name of W. H. Malloch who wrote a book called *The New Republic* who once maintained this, but I doubt if few could do so today.

No such differentiation of classes can be scientifically defended. There is a fundamental unity of mankind which, within limits, is increasingly recognized by men and women. Without wishing to preach to our good friend, and I hope he will excuse me if I sound patronizing, I would say that his associates—not him, but his associates in the Tory party—would be greatly helped if they studied the words and deeds of the Founder of Christianity who taught that all men were brothers and that we should help the poor because of their need and do so without any patronizing or any sense of false superiority. And if this seems too sentimental for those who relish the verbal felicities of the Book of Common Prayer, may I recall to them one of Immanuel Kant's categorical imperatives "Treat humanity, whether in thyself or in another, always as an end, never as a means." Or let them take as a guide for action their sturdy fellow countryman Jeremy Bentham's rule of "the greatest good for the greatest number," or be animated by the spirit of Albert Schweitzer's "Reverence for Life." Mr. Powell, I hope you will let me come to

England sometime and preach this gospel to the parliamentary constituencies of the Tory party.

Now the conservative worshipper of the market process may reject all this and may once again reverence market values. But I submit that such a society will be aesthetically ugly, morally barren, emotionally cold, and will lack the cohesive powers needed for survival in the world struggle.

The second great weakness of the market price system is its failure to distinguish between individual business cost and social cost. I am really surprised that so able a man as Mr. Powell does not seem to know of this distinction, or possibly, knowing of it, chooses for debating purposes to slur over it. For both English literature and political economy from Carlyle and Ruskin to Wells and Shaw and Hobson and Pigou are very explicit on this point. Thus let us hear Ruskin thunder once again that much of the so-called "weal—th" is really "ill—th" and then mentally fill in the specifics to his generality. Let us go back again and read Bernard Shaw's essay of 1886 of how the private gas works and grog shops could roll off great costs onto the public, to their own individual profit. And then let us study Pigou's *The Economics of Welfare* —coming as it does from that citadel of British neoclassical economics prior to Keynes, namely Cambridge University.

Consider for a moment the steel mill or power plant which burns coal with a high sulphur content and hence spews out poisonous smoke and fumes mixed in some cases with iron sulphites. This costs the firm less than would a higher grade of coal or improved devices to catch and utilize the smoke. But it throws upon the hundreds of thousands of housewives and families the labor and cost of trying to cleanse their clothes and homes from the stains of smoke and grime. And as we have found in this country, the smoke from the steel mills, oil refineries, and power plants blights crops and hurts farming as well as other manufacturing. It lowers real estate values and, most of all, it reduces the level of health, encourages respiratory disorders, and causes deaths. It not only causes a slow economic loss but also shortens life and hence violates Ruṣkin's rule which hard-boiled critics still neglect, namely that "there is no wealth but life."

And yet it is extraordinarily difficult to reduce this health hazard, as it also is to deal with the excessive exhaust poisons from automobiles and trucks. For the extra costs involved to the producers make them in general oppose corrective measures. While those on the receiving end collectively suffer a greater loss than those on the producing end gain, or avoid, this is not true of each individual taken separately. As a result, the general interest tends to be fragmented, diffused, and subordinated to the more restrictive special or producing interest.

The same contradiction exists in the case of water pollution, which has already brought once beautiful Lake Erie, so beloved by James Fenimore Cooper, to its

death and which now threatens the southern end of
Lake Michigan, so dearly beloved by millions of us
middle westerners. Only those who have been involved
in the attempt to save these lakes and to clean up noble
rivers like the Mississippi can fully appreciate the difficulties as industry throws its costs upon society and by
threatening either to move or to shut off growth frightens localities and sometimes even states into allowing
the wasteful and befouling practices to continue.

Apparently Mr. Powell thinks these dangers can be
overcome by straight out government prohibitions. But
to obtain such a prohibition over the opposition of the
interests in question is a very difficult matter, especially
in view of the fact that those who share Mr. Powell's
distrust of government action and exalt the market are
generally lined up in opposition to such government intervention. Moreover to make the prohibition stick, the
government will need the kind of enforcing machinery
which is also generally attacked by the economic conservatives as wasteful of both money and effort.

A third weakness of the system of market prices is
that it all too frequently grows out of monopoly and
highly imperfect competition rather than the pure competition postulated by the English classical economists
from Nassau William Senior to Alfred Marshall. Under
perfect competition with an unlimited number of producers, no one firm has any effect upon price, which is
made instead for them by the general conditions of
supply and demand and over which none of them has

any control. But the real conditions in manufacturing, finance, mining, and wholesale trade are very different. By 1920, the multitude of provincial banks described by Walter Bagehot in this book, *Lombard Street,* had been swallowed up in England by the Big Five without the economists either noticing it or protesting about it. Then came the further consolidation into one chemical company, Imperial Chemicals, a handful of armament firms, two or three cocoa companies, and cartels in textiles, steel, and engineering. England became the land of monopoly, not of competition. But the economists who sat upon battlements and scanned the industrial countryside gave no alarm, they slept at their posts.

An eloquent theoretical demonstration of the inherent consequences of all this, in abstract terms, was finally given by Joan Robinson in her *Economics of Imperfect Competition.* She proved, I think indisputably, that monopoly and imperfect competition inevitably restrict production and force upon the still largely competitive industries and services the burden of absorbing the unemployed labor and uninvested savings. Mr. Keynes therefore did not need to go as far afield as he did to find the reason for the long depression in British industry during the twenties and thirties.

The same influences have been at work in the United States, although we have been helped by the prior existence of the Sherman Antitrust and the Clayton Acts.

Now I know that Mr. Powell personally deprecates monopoly and restrictive practices and so far as I have

been able to follow his record in the British papers, I
believe that his personal record as a Parliamentarian is,
in this respect and in others, a highly honorable one.
But the point that I wish to make is that, with some
honorable exceptions such as Mr. Powell, the supporters
of his point of view have in practice promoted and run
the monoplies and cartels and in general resisted the efforts to restore and maintain competition. It is the same
here, as an examination of the votes in the House and the
Senate and in the Antitrust and Monopoly Subcommittee
reveal. It has been the verbal defenders of free enterprise
within the conservative coalition who have fought virtually every effort to make competition more effective
and monopoly less prevalent.

One way to extend competition in a very mild way is
of course to give greater information to consumers so
that they can better protect themselves, as well as to set
a minimum of ethical standards to which an industry is
expected to conform. But the correct labeling of foods
and drugs was opposed in the days of Upton Sinclair
and Harvey Wiley, as was the Securities Act a third of
a century ago in the days of Franklin Roosevelt. Stamped
indelibly on my mind is the opposition to my truth-in-
lending bill which merely provided that borrowers and
buyers should be told the truth about what the real
annual rates of interest were on the amounts actually
owed instead of this being covered up by a multitude of
devices. It was the so-called defenders of free enterprise
who opposed these efforts, as they did those of my friend

Estes Kefauver in the field of drugs, while it was those of us who were constantly being attacked as the enemies of free enterprise who fought to establish a greater degree of competition in which the buyer as well as the seller was to be safeguarded.

But there should be personal as well as commodity competition. Men should be judged by their works if society is to develop. Hereditary class distinctions are hostile to this. Under such a system, try as able men may, they will in general find themselves passed over in favor of those with favored parents, those who wear the old school tie, and those who have the approved accent— and one has only to look at the choice of leadership in the Conservative party to see how true this is—

MR. POWELL: The Democratic party?

SENATOR DOUGLAS: No, The Conservative party in England. [Laughter.] When these become the qualities which tip the scales of success, then leadership in industry and statecraft grows feeble, and honest effort is discouraged.

And yet it is Mr. Powell's party which throughout its long life has tried to maintain and strengthen these hereditary class distinctions and which uses the monarchy and the regency as its emotional stimulus. The Labor government in Great Britain is seeking to lessen these hereditary class distinctions, by abolishing the hereditary principle for the House of Lords. We are not free from these distinctions in this country. But we are not as burdened with them as are our British friends. Careers are more open to talents and this very fact accounts for much of our prosperity as well as for the basic dislike which the aristocratic sections of Europe have always felt towards us. I shall not reply to those groups in detail but I will quote some lines from our distinctive American poet, Walt Whitman.

> Do the older races falter
> Do they droop and end their lessons
> Wearied over there beyond the seas?
> We take up the task eternal
> And the burden and the message
> Pioneers, O Pioneers.

It is perhaps well to move towards the end on a seemingly minor note. Public enterprise can often engage in a gigantic venture which is ultimately productive but which by its sheer size and complexity frightens away private enterprise. An example of this was the decision of President Roosevelt to develop atomic power. The possibilities of success in the beginning were highly problematical. Roosevelt and the nation spent a billion dollars on it. If the venture had turned out badly, if the money had been wasted, or if an explosion had occurred, blowing up a portion of Chicago, Roosevelt's opponents would have been unmerciful in their criticism. And those who disbelieved in government enterprise would have cited the failure as proof positive that government officials had become dizzy with power and impelled to launch out on projects which no rational and hardheaded businessman would initiate. The experiment was however, as we know, a great technical success. It has revolutionized warfare and its mere possession in our hands has been a powerful deterrent in Europe to aggressive communism. What its ultimate effect will be upon the peace and security of the world is still uncertain. But the venture has been supremely successful within the political limits of modern society and it has also opened up a new world in its possible peaceful uses as well. Had all of this been left to private enterprise, it would never have been attempted or carried out. The costs were too great, the risks too fearsome, the longtime gains too far away and conjectural to justify private initiation and finance.

Of course, I know that there have been failures such as the effort to grow peanuts—ground nuts I think you call them—on a gigantic scale in Africa. Khrushchev's effort to transform Siberia into a corn-growing country has also apparently failed. But I submit that we have made a good overall record in this country.

Thus private industry would never have had the capital or the courage to develop the latent water power resources of the Tennessee Valley in the way TVA has done, nor would it have ventured out upon the coordinated development of the Columbia and its tributaries in the way that has been done publicly by our government. By a thoroughgoing river development, the entire fall of water can be used and pushed through a coordinated system of dams in a way that single dams could never do.

Similar economies have been effected in Ontario by the Hydro-Electric Authority of that province, which gave us lessons for many years which we refused to learn but which finally Congress and the great Robert Moses successfully put through. (We have a Moses in this country too, Mr. Powell.) I also count the system of REA cooperatives to have been a success in their effects on rural life. The advantages given through area coverage justify, in my judgment, the lower interest rates and tax advantages which the co-ops have been permitted to enjoy. Once given this start, most of the co-ops stand ready to pay the market rates of interest. But they could not have done so in the beginning and some favoritism was needed to get the system off the ground. The same principle applies also for the rural telephone cooperatives.

It is obvious that our country faces a real crisis in the problems of our cities and metropolitan areas. To deal with these we need a huge investment in housing for low-income families, and in civic necessities and amenities. Many billions of dollars will be required. With the money incomes of the poor as low as they are, this cannot be done profitably by private industry. The monetary income of the poor is so low that they cannot pay for decent housing. And yet the social by-products in reduced crime and reduced social disorder would be great. After last summer who can doubt that in the larger sense it would be a good investment.

There is moreover an alternative to purely state or purely individual action. This is cooperation or voluntary mutual action. While the cooperative movement has not taken as deep roots in this country as in the Scandinavian countries or in the retail trade of Great Britain, there has been great growth here in recent years. There are for example 18 million members in 23,000 local credit unions which now loan $9 billion to their members. This is one-ninth of the total amount of small loan installment credit. In addition there are 3.7 million members in farm marketing associations and 3.2 million in farm purchasing cooperatives. The turnover of the former is over $12 billion a year and of the latter more than $3 billion. There are just short of 4 million members of group health plans and nearly 12 million in co-op oriented insurance companies.

I have referred to the REA co-ops, which number 993 with 5.6 million members and $1 billion of annual sales. There are about 1,200 cooperative banks serving farming with total credits granted of over $7.5 billion.

We have been and still are weak in cooperatives for consumer goods. But there are 116 such bona fide co-operatives dealing with food and home supplies. They include 165,000 family members, or probably close to 700,000 individuals, and do an annual business of $160 million. I hope you will stop off in Chicago, Mr. Powell, and see our Hyde Park cooperative which my wife and I helped to start. She was very active in it for many years. In the initial year its total sales amounted to $3,500. But this last year sales were $6 million, for 10,000 members. Moreover, it paid a patronage dividend of 3.5 percent and has introduced a spirit of fraternity which is very precious. In addition, housing co-ops are developing rapidly, especially in New York and Detroit, and are now housing 165,000 families or probably close to three-quarters of a million members.

The cooperatives are therefore slowly becoming a third force. They have certain definite economic advantages, notably in assuring demand, reducing competitive expense, and enlisting the active interest and participation of their members. They temper and sweeten the asperities of competition and transform the fields in which they operate into agencies for mutual helpfulness.

They are subject to all the weaknesses which afflict imperfect human beings as they struggle to work together, whether in businesses or churches or political parties, or what-have-you. But they have many of the advantages of both private and state enterprise and hence can serve as a reconciliation of the individualistic and collectivist principles. They also give people a chance to take part in many fields of action which would otherwise be closed to them. Men and women therefore become participants and not pawns—not anonymous numbers, but active participants.

In conclusion, I submit that we should not be slavish followers of any one economic or social philosophy. While individual enterprise and competitive market price should be the guiding principle, there is room for some state and cooperative enterprise as well. Moreover, monopoly and quasi-monopoly should not be allowed to hide behind the false Halloween mask of competition, and government can and should try to see that competition is real, both as between producers and as between buyers and sellers. I submit also that society should be characterized by what the French economist, Charles Gide, and the sociologist, Emile Durkheim, used to characterize as the principle of solidarity, namely that the weak should be protected by the strong, that we seek to eliminate poverty and other social ills and that we recognize the state not as a devouring ogre but as one of the agencies through which man can lead the good and the better life.

Thank you very much. We pray for your conversion, Brother Powell.

We hope that when you go back, you will be less robust in your faith. And, frankly, I think that you don't belong in the Tory party. I think you're too good a man to be in the Tory party. We can't expect you to join the Labor party. But I do think you ought to take our membership in the British Liberal party.

DISCUSSION

FIRST SESSION

EMERSON SCHMIDT, Economic Consultant: I was a little surprised, Senator, that you didn't devote a little more time to what is called the new techniques of cost-benefit analysis or cost effectiveness. We all agree with these normal aspirations that you have outlined, but there are costs too. I wonder if you would tell us what your own experience was as a senator after the President pronounced in favor of this principle.

SENATOR DOUGLAS: Well, at the risk of being egotistical, let me tell you the experience that I had in the Defense Department. I had been convinced ever since 1951 that there was enormous waste in the Defense Department, but I could make no headway under Truman nor under Eisenhower.

There were a number of things that made me very suspicious. Eighty-six percent of the contracts, both in number and in dollars, were awarded by negotiated bidding in which there was no competition, only negotiation with a single supplier. They arranged cost-plus-fixed-fee contracts, and the percentage of cases in which the cost went up over and above the original estimate was very great. The people on the Renegotiation Board with whom I talked published analyses of many cases showing really extraordinary profits in supplies.

Then in the spring of 1960 I got possession of invoices for large numbers of purchases of common tools. I won't say how I got them, but I got them. We had the price riveted down. I got hold of physical specimens of these goods and then went out and matched that price, went to a hardware store and matched the screwdrivers, and other simple things. And in nearly every case we found a price which would be from three to six to ten times as great with the government purchasing wholesale in large quantities as I could purchase retail.

I brought forth this evidence on the floor of the Senate in July, 1960. The Defense Department became furious at this, and they came over to see me. I shall never forget it. They opened the door and in came about 15 officers. They sat there in a phalanx, with the silent intimidatory policy of the military. Fortunately I stood my ground and fortunately I had the invoices. They tried to find out how I got them. I wouldn't tell them.

They wouldn't admit they were wrong at all.

The election of 1960 turned out as we know, and McNamara was appointed Secretary of Defense. I wrote him a three-page memorandum citing this evidence and asking him to do certain things! First, to introduce a much larger share of competitive bidding. I said that if we in the city of Chicago purchased goods the way the Defense Department was purchasing goods, the whole country would have screamed and would have tried to put our people in jail.

Furthermore, they would be buying goods identical to those which they were scrapping. At the same time they would be buying on the one hand and scrapping on the other, instead of pooling their supplies. Sometimes even the same service would buy at the same time that it was scrapping.

I became convinced that they were overbuying, that their disposal of surplus was faulty, and that there was a whole series of other abuses.

I didn't think much was going to come of it, but Mc-Namara immediately replied, and he invited [Representative Thomas] Curtis of Missouri, Republican, who had been interested in the same thing, and a number of other members of the Armed Services Committee to meet with him. We met with him every three months for two-and-a-half years. He closed in on these things, going over each item. And he finally produced his figures, that he had made savings which he claimed of four-and-a-quarter billion dollars a year, and later it went up to six billion.

Now, I'm not an expert on accounting, but it looked good to me. He was the first Secretary of Defense who had really made economies.

He did not introduce purely advertised competitive bidding; he did introduce competitive negotiated bidding in which instead of one firm getting the contract, he would get six or seven bidding against each other. And he introduced a system of sharing savings, rather than cost-plus-fixed-fee. If the contract was fulfilled for less than the negotiated amount, the contractor would get a portion of the amount saved. I think there is no doubt that he did cut costs. I think he is a great Secretary of Defense, the best this nation has ever had.

As to the application of this principle to other branches of the government, I don't know. The President has credited me with starting that, but I certainly didn't follow it up. On the TFX contract I don't know what the facts are. I can only say that everything that I did see made me feel that he is the first man we have ever had there who paid any attention to these subjects and who was not afraid of the contractors or the procurement officials.

There was another thing I wanted. I wanted a centralized purchasing agency for all the armed services. We got that. And that made real savings. We had fewer people employed in the consolidated service than we had in the four separate supply services.

But on the intricacies of this cost benefit analysis, all the mathematical business of one and the other, I don't pretend to be an expert. I can only say that on what I tested, what I know about, Secretary McNamara did very well.

GEORGE HAGEDORN, National Association of Manufacturers: I think perhaps I am pursuing the point that Emerson Schmidt brought up, but let me put it this way. As we listened to you, Senator, I think all of us were groping to discern the framework of analysis in which you spoke of each of these items of federal activity or government activity, what your basis was for deciding in each case whether this was a proper form of activity, whether the degree to which it was being carried on was the right degree or not.

And I wound up still puzzled as to just how you made that classification. You spoke in defense, for example, of government expenditures in this country for public libraries. You said public libraries are a fine thing, they are related to continuing education. I don't think anybody in this group would want to attack the idea of having public libraries. On the other hand, I don't think any of us here would agree with spending 95 percent of the national income to support public libraries.

Now, just how do you make the decision as to what the right amount is? That wasn't clear at all in any part of your discussion, with all due respect.

SENATOR DOUGLAS: Well, a good many of these judgments have to be qualitative. In the case of public libraries, it is an expenditure of approximately $2.50 a year per person. I'm not frightened by spending $2.50 a year per person for public libraries. Perhaps someone else will be. But that is exacly what it is.

MR. HAGEDORN: Then you have no criterion that you can describe in at all precise terms for how you draw the line?

SENATOR DOUGLAS: Well, I can't get it down to one-hundredth of 1 percent, but I can get it to a point where you can make a judgment. Let me take the super-

sonic plane which is the darling of so many people. It is
going to cost probably at the minimum $4 billion. It is
going to cut a noise swath of from 35 to 50 miles. They
are trying to cover up on these Oklahoma City tests
the large number of panes of glass broken and so
forth. I should not expect that initially you could fly
the supersonic plane over the country, not initially. If
they could get people conditioned to it, perhaps they
could, but not to begin with. So it will be primarily for
international flights in the beginning, from California to
Hawaii and the Orient, from the Atlantic Coast to Britain and the Continent.

Now, the speed will be 1,800 miles per hour as compared to 600 miles. This will reduce the time by about
three or four hours. The people who will be able to
utilize it will be the wealthy people, what I refer to as
the international jet set, and I think that's right.

You would have to, since they have much greater
speed on takeoffs and landings, you would have to have
the airports farther out. In a slang language, you ain't
seen nothing yet. Dulles will have to move still farther
out.

The one thing that I regret, the only vote that I would
change if I were in the Senate again, I should have voted
against Dulles. I would have voted in favor of Friend-
ship over Dulles Airport.

I really think that if you take that supersonic air
transport, the quantitative arguments are all against it.
The ultimate costs are going to be very great; the bene-

fits given will be for a relatively small number. You will have hidden costs of putting your airfields farther out. The noise factor is going to be very great.

That may not be a cost benefit analysis, but you get some facts which contribute.

The same thing with putting a man on the moon. I have talked with any number of military men who say there is no military advantage in putting a man on the moon, that you can hit every point on the earth's surface that you want now from the earth's surface, particularly with the submarine, the nuclear submarine. Or, if you want to bombard Russia from the skies, you can do it from a low-height orbit. There is no military value in getting on the moon.

The scientists tell me there is no scientific value, that you can get everything you want by instruments. About three-quarters of the cost of space exploration are involved in getting this man on the moon and back. So I conclude, very frankly, that this prestige race with the Russians led us into expenditures of at least $3.5 billion of the $5 billion that we are spending on space each year.

To me that isn't worth it. When this first came up, I protested. I asked [David] Bell, who was then Director of the Budget, "How much is this going to cost?" This was years ago. He said, "$20 billion." I said, "It's not worth it."

And immediately a senator who is a friend of mine spoke up and said they didn't think the subsidy to Alexander Graham Bell for a telegraph line between here and

Baltimore was worth it, but it turned out favorably. I looked that up, and it was a subsidy of $50,000. Well, $50,000 was worth more in the 1840s than it is today. But the expenses are not commensurate.

STEPHEN HORN, Brookings Institution: Senator, following up on this PPBS and its application—

SENATOR DOUGLAS: I don't know what that is.

MR. HORN: Well, the planning-program-evaluating, this McNamara-Rand Corporation-spawned system which is now applied to the civilian end of the government. What are your thoughts as to the role of Congress in evaluating the goals of the executive branch, especially on this topic of how big government should be?

Obviously you have Congress as sort of an administrative ombudsman to help the citizen against the bureaucracy. You've got Congress still with a legislative function. But you've also got it as a consensus or evaluator of the public policy that is mostly suggested by the executive. Yet within Congress the various substructures, like the appropriations committees and some of the substantive committees, object to the PPBS system because they really don't want to deal with programs in terms of goals. They would rather deal with them in terms of increments as to how many more people you want a year, how many more typewriters you want a year, etc. In other words, they would rather look at the individual trees than at the forest.

I wonder what your thoughts are as to how one can practically get some organizational reform in Congress so that there can be some will expressed on these basic value judgments as to how big the government should be.

SENATOR DOUGLAS: I don't pretend to be an expert on that. I can say that I would hate to see the time come when Congress did not exercise the power of basic decision for expenditures. I suppose everyone tends to become enamored of the institution in which he serves. But I do not believe in the administrative state. I think that can get the taxpayers and the people committed to many things that are not in the public interest. This is one reason I favor the American system of committee hearings, committee review, rather than more or less accepting a budget and voting it up or down.

Nevertheless, let me say that I recognize the weaknesses in the present appropriating process. It is too slow. I suppose one reason that I am rather critical about the way it is carried out is the composition of the appropriations committees. All the power is going to the appropriations committees. This is the center of power, appropriating money—this and military affairs. People interested in the exercise of naked power want to get on the appropriations committees.

I favor governmental expenditures for human welfare, unless they are wasteful. But you don't get many people who believe in that sort of thing who go for the appropriations committees, or who get on them.

For a brief period of time I was a member of the Committee on Committees of my party in the Senate.

And it was almost impossible for us to get what we called a progressive on the Appropriations Committee. The southern conservatives predominated completely, or the western public works men. They have an alliance with each other, really. They fight with each other on the surface, but the mountain states and the south are right in together. They won't admit it, but they play ball with each other. It is almost impossible for the Democrats from the eastern industrial states or the midwestern industrial states to get into the seats of power.

So you get the most conservative elements in both parties on the appropriations committees, and they just love to take it out of education and poverty and welfare and all these things.

I was really talking as much against them as I was against Enoch Powell when I made my remarks.

ROGER FREEMAN, The Hoover Institution on War, Revolution and Peace, Stanford University: Senator, you mentioned that Mr. McNamara is the first Secretary of Defense who was aiming for and did achieve major savings.

I wonder whether we can go beyond that and say that he also is the only cabinet officer who has not been trying to increase his congressional appropriations, who has consistently refused to spend major funds appropriated by Congress and who has been trying to hold down the appropriations by Congress? The question is whether his title should be Secretary of Defense, Secretary Against Defense, or Secretary for Disarmament.

You referred to expenditures for welfare, for education, for urban programs. You indicated we really ought to be spending more on these purposes because the American people want more education and need more education.

Can the amount of expenditures be equated with the results? Are there some measuring sticks by which we can measure what the return is? We have always assumed in the past, at least most people have assumed, that input is about the only measuring stick.

Now, we have some measuring sticks that can be used and would be used in any other field. As the funds multiplied many times, so did the social ills that these programs promised and were expected to reduce.

As to the urban programs, earlier this year the mayor of Detroit, speaking to the Senate subcommittee under Senator [Joseph] Clark, pointed out that his city had been free of the unrest which had characterized many other cities, because Detroit was an example of a city with programs to which other cities could look if they wanted to avoid riots. We all know what happened after that.

New Haven has received far more in federal funds than any other city. In fact, close to $1,000 per capita, which is more than any other city could do.

SENATOR DOUGLAS: $800 per capita.

MR. FREEMAN: Yes. Now, it is apparent that we couldn't do as much for all cities at this point as was done for New Haven, because it would mean $100 billion a year, which at this point still is beyond our capacity. Now, if $100 billion a year could not prevent the kind of unrest which we experienced this year in New Haven, if the same program is applied, what makes us think that by multiplying the funds we could prevent unrest somewhere else, if more than $800 a year for New Haven did not prevent it?

Another example I would like to quote, Senator, is education. We all want better education. We have had several major reports just this past year. The biggest one, certainly in terms of expenditures, was the Coleman Report which cost a million-and-a-half dollars and covered 400,000 children. It found, to the great surprise of its originators, that there is almost no statistical correlation between expenditure per pupil and scholarly achievement of the pupil.

In a report which the Office of Education published about three months ago on Title I of the Education Act of 1965, which was enacted because Congress was concerned about the lack among many of the poorer children of the basic skills—we found that of the tests that were taken by hundreds of thousands of children in 19 different subjects from word comprehension to arithmetic reasoning, that in 10 of the 19 tests children who had gone through the program were slightly ahead, and in nine tests they were behind. In other words, the net result was just about zero.

The third example is contained in a recent report of the U.S. Commission on Civil Rights which has a chapter on so-called compensatory programs which, of course, have been growing very rapidly. This report finds, after studying over 20 compensatory programs from New York to Berkeley and from Syracuse to Pittsburgh, that there has been virtually no improvement in the actual scholarly achievements in the "three Rs" of the pupils who participated.

My question is: If these are the results so far, is that encouragement to spend more? Or should we accept the fact that absence of results has no impact on our thinking and on the decisions of Congress? If the government had produced the Edsel, the car which Ford started a few years ago with disastrous results, it would still be making it, turning out large quantities and giving them away.

SENATOR DOUGLAS: Well, what you say is certainly to be considered. I haven't seen those education studies. I have given some thought to New Haven and Detroit. I think there is no doubt that in both New Haven and Detroit the money expended was not used to any significant degree for the benefit of the poor.

If you go through New Haven, you will find that what was done was primarily to build up the city of New Haven around the Yale Yard, to put in good hotels and buildings around the Yale Yard so that the Yale alumni when they came home could be housed in a better place than the Hotel Taft, which was built in 1909. All this made the city of New Haven look much better.

There has been no public housing constructed there since 1954. And when the riots broke out, Dick Lee, who is a good man, a good honest man, made a very truthful statement. According to the *New York Times,* he said he thanked God there had been no ugly buildings such as public housing erected in New Haven when he had been mayor. He gloried in it.

They did build a model neighborhood school. But that was about the only thing done for the poor. We held a public hearing there, and I felt there was a great deal of hatred underneath the surface and a general feeling that the poor had not benefited in any significant degree from the improvement.

In Detroit I think this is completely clear. And [Mayor] Cavanaugh is a very frank fellow. He said that we have failed in Detroit to make the poor feel that we want to help them. He said this has been our failure. And if you go into the urban renewal projects, what were they? There was one to help Wayne University, including a stadium. There was a hospital complex which was helped. There was a slum which was replaced by a garden apartment where the rents were very high.

Millions were spent on these projects, tens of millions. But the people didn't benefit very much.

I don't say this was the main cause for the riots. By no means. There are deeper, historical causes, three hundred years of subordination of the Negro. But I do say this was an accelerating cause. It reminds me of David Copperfield. You may remember that when Copperfield came up to London the stagecoach driver would take him into an inn and there the stagecoach driver would eat an enormous meal. He would order for Copperfield but Copperfield wouldn't get a chance to eat. The driver took it all. And they followed this pattern all the way up to London. Each successive driver would order a big meal for Copperfield and then eat it himself. And so Copperfield got the reputation of having this enormous appetite. When he arrived in London, they scolded him for having such an appetite.

It is true, I think, that a lot of these expenditures have been misdirected and have not gone to the intended project. One of the discouraging things is the way in which the well-to-do muscle in on the benefits of the poor.

MICHAEL BERNSTEIN, Senate Labor Committee: I would concede that there is probably a tendency of what you refer to as conservatives to resist almost automatically programs of welfare, education, and so on. But don't you think there is an analogous tendency on the part of the proponents of such programs to oversell their future potentialities? I think of the pacifist who says "You must not use violence because it is immoral to do so, and, what is more, if you don't use violence, you will also win the fight." The two don't necessarily go together. You may lose the fight and it may still nevertheless be moral not to use violence.

The proponents, it seems to me, of a good many welfare programs, just as Mr. Freeman has indicated, have a tendency when they push a program to make predictions of what its beneficial effects will be, beneficial effects which couldn't possibly be attained, certainly to the degree which they sell them.

SENATOR DOUGLAS: I think that's true, Mike. I think there is always a tendency for people to overstress the arguments in favor of what they believe and to be overoptimistic. I don't think that is peculiar to our people, but I think it is a general tendency running through all groups.

If I can just come back to the education question. Some of you may know that I tried to work out a production equation, making production a function of labor and capital, which seemed to work out pretty well. But it didn't work out for the period from 1930 to the 1950s where production rose more rapidly than either the quantity of labor or capital relatively.

And my colleague Professor Schultz at Chicago—I don't think he is prejudiced in these matters—worked out an equation in which he made education a third factor in production and seemed to prove what I thought was true, that expenditures on education, however imperfectly carried out, have an effect in increasing the net productivity of the American economy. I cannot believe that ignorance is productive, nor can I believe that ability to profit from education is confined to the prosperous. And I submit that the rate of progress that we have made in this country has been due in part not merely to the ratio of natural resources and capital to population, but also to the broad extension of education.

You may dispute that. It may be faith based on imperfect knowledge. It probably is. But I submit that it has worked out pretty well, that the economies which have doubted the ability of average men and women to benefit from education have been relatively lethargic economies. The Moslem economies are relatively stationary economies. Ours are not.

NORMAN TURE, National Bureau of Economic Research: I don't think anyone in this room would dispute your assertion that the level of educational attainment has something to do with the rate at which total output can increase through time. But that's not really the issue. No one here, I think, will dispute with you the desirability of having an educational establishment in American society, nor that that establishment should grow.

The problem that we really must deal with concerns the extent to which valuable resources are committed to expanding the size of that establishment. Those resources have alternative uses. They are enormously valuable and their opportunity costs therefore are enormously high. The problem that we really have to come to grips with is: What is the mechanism we are to use to determine at what point further expansion should be moderated? Not cut off, but moderated.

SENATOR DOUGLAS: Well, $35 billion spent on education in the years 1965-66. How would you have altered that?

MR. TURE: I don't know that I would have altered

it at all. And I don't think really that that is at issue—

SENATOR DOUGLAS: I think it is.

MR. TURE:—between you and me or the other people present, sir. Nor do I really think that is the issue that separates so-called liberals from so-called conservatives.

Conservatives don't say that there should not be an educational establishment nor that that establishment should not grow, nor do they say that public functions are evil, nor do they say that public functions should not expand as the economy expands.

What they do is to express a vague and non-rigorously determined concern about the fact that they can observe, as you can and have observed more effectively than most people have, a great many public programs, the justification for which just never can be established. You express some considerable concern about the space program and about the supersonic transport program. I happen to share your biases here. And I think that these are programs of such a nature that, using the techniques of cost-benefit analysis, it may or may not be possible to establish that they aren't very good bets.

But there are all sorts of other programs where, whether or not you can measure the cost, it is very difficult to come up with an objective measure of benefits. What typically happens is that those who are invested with those programs tend to attribute to them a sufficient volume of benefits to justify them at *any* rational or reasonable discount rate.

SENATOR DOUGLAS: Believe me, this question of

expenditures on education cannot be taken for granted, because in the localities this issue goes on all the time, the battle is waged all the time. And it is waged in the states, as to the degree of state aid. It is waged in the federal government, as to whether there shall be federal aid or not. And you say these things are taken for granted, that everybody agrees with them. Everybody doesn't agree when it comes down to these questions.

I was really challenging Mr. Powell, and I'll challenge anyone here, to tell what you would do with that $35 billion of public money. I think the average expenditures are somewhere between $550 to $600 per pupil per year. That may be off, but I think that is about it.

Are you going to increase total expenditures at the rate of $550 per pupil as the number of pupils increases? Are you going to cut this? Are you going to give the same added amount to children in the suburbs coming from cultivated homes that you do to children in the slums coming from families that have been field hands in Mississippi, living in one room, never having a chance to read a book?

MR. TURE: Should that $35 billion figure have been $70 billion or $105 billion?

SENATOR DOUGLAS: I challenge Mr. Powell to say that it shouldn't be $35 billion.

JOHN MIDGELY, *The Economist* of London: It does seem to me that this particular problem of how you price everything is a problem inherent in your system of government. If you have a system of government which is, say like the French, only perhaps a little more perfect, a little more scientific, but broadly like the French where you have a specially-trained elite running the country from a central point in which they are in charge of the entire decision-making process subject to incursions and influences from public opinion, but essentially in charge, presumably it is theoretically possible to put price tags on various public goods and relate them to each other and divide up the available resources. It is even possible to put a price tag on the available resources. Then one knows perfectly well that the Mirage [French bomber] is worth so many billion and the lycee is worth so many billion when you relate these things.

You have a system in which money is apportioned for public goods, broadly speaking, to the extent that groups and movements of opinion in the country are able to bring voices, pressure, muscle to bear in their favor and thus get away with it. And thus the distribution of the public expenditures, very broadly, represents the equation of popular pressures. And I'm using "popular" in the very broad sense, which does include General Motors.

In the course of justifying a particular scheme, mobilizing support for it and bringing pressure to bear—arguing down the other side—it is almost inevitable that the proponents of the scheme will claim for it a lot of benefits which are not strictly relevant to the scheme itself. It seems to me always a little spooky—I can understand how it happens—when people have to justify a housing scheme or an education scheme or a hospital scheme by saying "This will make people happy" and "Then you won't have any troubles from them," "This is a way of curing riots," and so on. But a lot of things are always promised for a particular scheme which need not be promised.

Broadly speaking, you improve the schools so that children will be better educated, because it is a good thing that little blighters should be better educated, not necessarily so that they won't burn the town down. And right round the spectrum. You can even apply this to foreign aid, you see.

The people who really thought out the foreign aid scheme would not of themselves in bed at night have said: "If you give all this money to France to reconstruct her economy, you will consequently get a French government which will support the foreign policy of the United States." The rationale behind the American effort to help reconstruct Western Europe after the war was basically perhaps something much more simple and much more pertinent to what was actually being done. You wanted the reconstruction of Western Europe because you didn't want Western Europe to be in a mess, roughly.

SENATOR DOUGLAS: Basically I think what is dividing us is that some of you think the experts could do better than a democracy. And this is always a tendency of educated people, because they expect to be amongst the bureaucrats who make the decisions. So that they have a bias in favor of either bureaucratic or administrative decision rather than popular decision.

With all the faults of the appropriating process and all the faults of the taxing process, which are very tremendous, I would trust the imperfect judgments of the representatives of the people to those of the bureaucracy, a self-perpetuating bureaucracy, whether of France or Great Britain, or a Mohammedan state or the Chinese intelligentsia.

I suppose you come down to a judgment, a value judgment. I just happen to be that way and some of you happen to be the other way. I can just say that on the whole the American system has shown great vitality. The intellectuals can poke fun at it, but it has the power of strength and it has the power of endurance.

We went to the Rocky Mountains on the initiative of American frontiersmen, I'll quote an entirely irrational statement by Pascal which would infuriate the statisticians. Pascal was a great mathematician, but he was also a mystic and he saw deeply into things. He wrote one line, amongst many, which was very good. He said: "The heart has reasons which reason knows not of."

HARVEY SEGAL, *Washington Post*: Senator Douglas, would you care to comment on current congressional concern over the growth of federal spending? Where is this fight, in your opinion, going to lead?

SENATOR DOUGLAS: Who should do the cutting?

MR. SEGAL: Well, do you think there is going to be any cutting? How do you interpret all this?

SENATOR DOUGLAS: I think there should be, most

certainly. But probably it will not be in the areas that I think should be cut.

I think we ought to cut some on highways, we ought to cut our space effort, we ought to cut on the supersonic airliner. I would like to cut on the subsidies to private airlines, shipbuilders and ship operators and the $125 million a year which we hand out to the wealthy corporations and individuals that have private planes and get privileges for almost nothing.

JAMES STEINER, Chamber of Commerce: Going back to the title of the forum, How Big Should Government Be, I would like to ask the question, How big should it be in terms of percentage of national income?

You have mentioned that we are spending 30 percent of GNP and 37 percent of national income for all levels of government.

In percentage figures shouldn't it be 40 percent or 50 percent? What line would you draw in this kind of a measurement.

SENATOR DOUGLAS: I would not be as omniscient on this subject as my old friend Colin Clark who said that a country was doomed if it spent over 25 percent. Quite the contrary. America since 1960 has been going forward more rapidly I think than any other industrial country in the world. So I can only say that, judged by results, our going above 25 percent has not created the havoc that Clark so confidently predicted.

MR. MIDGELY: Excuse me, sir. But doesn't the level

go up, the permissible level go up as the country gets richer?

SENATOR DOUGLAS: I suppose so. But Clark gave his percentage as an absolute figure, absolute spending. He's supposed to be the greatest statistician in England.

MR. MIDGELY: I thought he was the greatest statistician in Australia. [Laughter.]

SENATOR DOUGLAS: The greatest statistician in Australia also happens to be the greatest statistician in England.

MR. STEINER: Could I just put another dimension on this. Sharing your concern about both private and public bureaucracy and admitting Mr. Freeman's points, which are quite apt, that various federal programs passed in the thirties have not really met the intended need, what are your thoughts about having the national government in various selective domestic fields set a minimum goal nationwide and then applying the Heller-Peckman Plan formula, using the federal government as a revenue-raising source, setting these goals, turning over operations on a decentralized basis to the state or city governments in the country who are close to the problems, where they could perhaps feel the pressure of the poor a little more ably than somebody sitting in the Department of Housing and Urban Development can in Washington?

SENATOR DOUGLAS: How much will the Negroes of Mississippi get of it, or the Negroes in Alabama, or how much will the city dwellers in New York city or Chicago get?

Formerly with the legislatures dominated by the rural regions, cities knew they wouldn't get much, because in the apportionment of state funds the cities were discriminated against.

Well, we got a Supreme Court decision, thank God; despite the efforts of some of my colleagues and the conservatives of the Senate, we defeated the effort to abort the so-called one man-one vote decision. But what happened? It gave political power to the suburbs, in much greater measure than to the cities, and the suburbs seem to dislike the cities just as much as the rural regions did. So that the cities are still encompassed about by their enemies.

I don't want to turn these funds over to the states and give them carte blanche on methods of apportionment. We've got to get some methods of apportionment which will reflect needs, a much more subtle formula on need which will also reflect the degree to which local governments and state governments are trying to meet needs.

MR. STEINER: But nobody has suggested you turn them over carte blanche. They're saying put in standards to avoid exactly the problem you very aptly point out as far as discrimination against Negroes is concerned.

SENATOR DOUGLAS: That's about what we are trying to do on education now, have the state expend the funds, subject to these, as you say, minimum standards. I wouldn't be opposed to that.

I am opposed to block grants, which is what Heller originally wanted, without federal controls. As a matter of fact, Seligman proposed this a half century or 60-70 years ago. He proposed that the federal government should levy an income tax and apportion it to the states according to an apportionment formula. I think that is, on the whole, good. But there are shoals ahead and dangers ahead.

MR. STEINER: Senator, the conditions which you fear, of course, in the apportionment of funds do not exist at the present time. I would like to relate this to two statements recently made in the press. One appeared in *U.S. News & World Report*, quoting Mr. [Floyd] Mc-Kissick, the Negro leader. When asked what the Negroes want, he said essentially this: "We want all you have and all you expect to get." Now, this is one view which perhaps may be a minority view of a minority.

But this week Mr. [the Rev. Martin Luther] King, another Negro leader, estimates that the need is for $20 billion a year to be spent on behalf of the poor people. Specifically, if Mr. King were to prevail, how could this money be spent usefully, with consideration to the record which the gentleman from The Hoover Institution has indicated, that compensatory programs have had no impact on scholarly achievements and that high levels of spending in such cities as Detroit and New Haven have not created conditions which have avoided riots?

How can we spend whatever the liberals want to spend

in addition to what is being spent and have these funds used successfully for advancing people?

SENATOR DOUGLAS: Well, first let me say that I think it is true that as long as the military expenditures continue at the level which they now are, it will be impossible to increase appreciably the expenditures for welfare, because we are doing well to hold on to what we have.

If we could ever get a quasi-peaceful world, there would be a great release of funds both for private expenditure and public expenditure. In some cases private expenditure will be more productive, and in certain other cases public expenditure would be more productive.

But I'm not for $20 billion now in view of the military situation. And I can understand the opposition which many people, who give the domestic situation extremely high priority have to the war.

DON GREEN, Chairman, Washington Chapter, Americans for Democratic Action: I'm Don Green, Chairman, Washington ADA. That's Americans for Democratic Action.

SENATOR DOUGLAS: I'm a member of the ADA too.

MR. GREEN: I know that. I thought you might like to see a friendly face. The one thing which I found strangely missing from the discussion tonight is any mention of the needs which must be served, any quantitative measure of how large the needs are. We have talked about inputs and outputs and wasteputs, but nothing about the kind of job that has to be done.

Most of the government programs with which I am familiar were initiated and have grown as an attempt to solve existing problems, usually problems which have been long standing problems, not new problems. Government, unfortunately, is not imaginative enough, intellectually or politically, to be able to initiate programs which anticipate problems. We are always reacting rather than acting.

I think an excellent example is the present air pollution problem which certainly is going to grow into an air pollution crisis. I find it hard to see how, without some very vast federal regulatory air pollution control program, we are going to get the automobile industry to stop manufacturing automobiles which pollute the environment. There is also the whole rather large program of oversell, the manufacturing and selling of more automobiles than are needed, of inefficiently-designed automobiles and automobiles which continue to make this problem grow.

Now, I think my question is really not directed at you, Senator, but perhaps at some of the other gentlemen who are here: How are we going to solve the air pollution problem without a large federal regulatory program? How will the industry police itself?

MR. TURE: May I reply to that very briefly?

SENATOR DOUGLAS: Yes, sure.

MR. TURE: I think it is a worthwhile effort for us

always to try to identify problems. But the mere identification does not mean either that we know how to solve them or that the federal government can solve them for us.

SENATOR DOUGLAS: Well, I can't keep out of that fight, because I live by the shores of Lake Michigan, and we have the states of Indiana and Illinois adjacent to each other. We in Illinois have not done too well, but not too badly on the pollution of the water. The state of Indiana has done miserably in Lake county, with the steel mills and oil refineries dumping all kinds of polluted water into the lake. This pollutes the whole lake, including the water for Illinois, as well as the water for Michigan.

The state of Indiana refuses to move ahead. Too expensive. The industries in Indiana won't move. What are you going to do? The *Chicago Tribune* has never been noted as a paper advocating governmental action in preference to private action, or federal action in preference to state action. I think they have properly come out and said that in these matters you have to have federal standards, not merely state standards.

Take another case. We've got a pretty good steel company down opposite St. Louis, but it pollutes the air; the air is terrible. The prevailing winds are from the west so that Missouri doesn't get much of it, except when there is an east wind. But the little city in question doesn't dare to require standards, the county doesn't dare require standards, lest the steel company move. This threat is used all the time as a weapon against local government or against state government: if you don't do this, we'll get out.

Get out where? Get out to some place where the standards are slack. It's going on all the time on air pollution, on pollution of water, on many other things. In the old days it was the cheap labor supply. Now it's not that entirely, but also something much more than that.

MR. MIDGELY: Is that the real reason, sir? Can a steel complex really move just to save a bit of expenditure on pollution?

SENATOR DOUGLAS: Well, they use it as a weapon. And there are some companies or industries which could move. You're quite right, in some instances. The localities, however, often don't dare call the bluff.

MR. HAGEDORN: May I make another comment on the subject raised by the gentleman from the ADA? Of course if we make a list of needs, whether it is public needs or of our personal individual needs, it is an endless list. We have to face the fact that society in general and we as individuals have only limited resources for satisfying all those needs. So that using our resources for anything that may be on your list or my list has an opportunity cost, as someone said earlier. The only way we can solve this is by making a list of the priorities. We can't do everything that is on your list of needs.

SENATOR DOUGLAS: That's right.

MR. HAGEDORN: Maybe on your list of priorities, correcting air pollution and water pollution rates very high. Maybe it rates at the top. But you still have to face the fact that if you are using up resources, they have to be resources that you could have used for something else.

I have been listening all night to try to get some help in my own thinking as to just how we can all get together and make a list of priorities that we can all agree on. I don't know whether we have come to any conclusions at all tonight on that subject.

Each of us has kind of introduced his own pet topics and intimated at least that they ought to be near the top of the list of priorities. But as for any general intellectual basis for establishing a list itself, we haven't gotten much further than we were when we came in.

MR. FREEMAN: Senator, you were asked whether $35 billion was too much for education, too little, or just about enough. I do not believe that anybody can answer that question as it is phrased.

But what we can do, I believe, and should do, is this. The city of New York is presently spending, about $1,000 per pupil, and in some schools it is spending more. We can measure how much the actual achievement is or the progress is of a pupil in any particular school over a year. We can measure how much progress is achieved, for example, in Utah, which spends less than half that much. We can measure among the almost 50 million pupils in this country what is achieved for a certain expenditure and how it is spent.

And I believe that any enterprise which spends $35

billion a year can afford and should measure and compare input and output. By output in this case I mean the progress of the children in skills and knowledge.

I think we could find an answer as to why many schools spend larger amounts and achieve little and other schools spend far less but achieve more. I think this could give us an indication of how much to spend and how to spend it.

Any private enterprise which would not do so would sooner or later fail. Why shouldn't we do that in government? That could give us some yardsticks.

SENATOR DOUGLAS: I would not object to that. But to take the specifics of your figures, I think you will find that the school districts which spend $1,000 a pupil are not in the cities. They are in the affluent suburbs. And these decisions are made by people with incomes over $10,000 a year, $15,000 a year, or $20,000 a year, decisions which they make for their own children. They decide this is worthwhile. The expenditures per child inside the cities, and particularly inside the slum districts, are very much less than this.

MR. FREEMAN: I'm sorry, Senator, but in recent years, if you follow it, you will find that the highest expenditures are in some of the slum districts, particularly in New York city.

In Chicago they are higher in the slum districts than in the other districts. And regardless of where it is, we would still be able to measure and establish some correlation between the amount of expenditure, the type of expenditure, how it is done, and what progress they have achieved. That ought to give us some indication. Regardless of what the results will be, we could learn something from it.

SENATOR DOUGLAS: Well, first let me say that I certainly want to see those figures. If you would send them to me, I would be very grateful. If I am wrong, I will admit it. But this conflicts directly with what I thought I had found out about the Chicago expenditures and the North Shore expenditures.

There is one other thing. We don't say that education is everything. When you get enormous numbers of people who are disadvantaged, whose parents have been disadvantaged for generations, you're not going to undo all of this in a day or a year or a decade. It's going to be a long affair.

I hope that we have never promised that we are going to make America over overnight. The question is: What is the long-run course upon which we want to embark? Is it in the development of people or purely in the development of material resources? Is it purely that?

Now, as I say, it comes down to faith. I believe that ultimately the development of people is best. We can justify it in part on the grounds that people are creative factors in production. But also we can justify it on the ground: What is the end of life? Is it merely the accumulation of material things or is it the development of human personalities? To me, people as such are the ends, not merely the means. Kant was right. And this introduces a dimension for which the student of input and output, physical indexes of production, has no instruments.

You have got me started now. I'm going to quote poetry. I'm going to quote Browning. "All the world's rough thumb and finger failed to plumb."

WILLIAM COPENHAVER, House Government Operations Committee: Senator, the question of the debate has been How Big Government Should Be. From all the discussion we have had this evening, the question is unanswerable. Keeping in mind the finite sums of money that we have to spend at any one time, keeping in mind the priorities that we have to seek to develop, and the cost-benefit ratios and the different programs which we all desire to push, the problem really is that we have a constantly shifting criterion, shifting need, where perhaps in one instance the impetus comes from local government, as in Wisconsin many years ago in social security; a second kind might come from the federal government on the question of water or air pollution; a third kind may come from private enterprise in perhaps taking over some unemployment work programs or slum renewal programs. Perhaps in one instance the federal government will initiate a program or create the impetus to be picked up by private enterprise or by local government. Therefore we are constantly having this shifting. And we should recognize the need for this shifting back and forth.

All of us, conservatives and liberals alike, get locked

into one solution to a problem, whether it be the federal government, or state government, or private enterprise. We don't realize that the ultimate goal is the most efficient solution to a problem.

SENATOR DOUGLAS: Well, I would agree in general with that, but I think there is a danger of falling into pure empiricism, of having no central philosophy, so that each individual decision presents itself as isolated from the whole set of decisions. I go back to what I said at the end, that I think human values, though difficult to measure, should be the supreme values.

SECOND SESSION

STEPHEN HORN, Brookings Institution: I am interested in your thoughtful comments but I do have a couple of questions perhaps that deal in the nitty gritty. I think you assume more rationality for government decisions or even market decisions than it is fair to say in reality exists. I wonder two things:

One—what your thoughts are on the proposition that decisions are not made in the rational sense and looking at the total universe, as you seem to imply. But instead, when a decision is made, you see only a small part as a decision maker; there are pressures within society. Let's talk about defense. The fact that a plant exists in a certain state and we might just as well give that plant the business, say the TFX in Texas, or the fact that there is a problem of unemployment in an area—there are political realities to be faced in decision making as there are economic realities.

My other question is about making economic judgments. Certainly the money system is a good one, but I am sure you would be the first to say it's not the perfect one. It is just one of the few systems we have.

The question is: How do you place a realistic value on something like wilderness? In our country we have the wilderness legislation that would isolate huge areas—

A VOICE: Greenery.

MR. HORN: —yes, well, huge areas of the primeval forest for the enjoyment of future generations.

How do you put a value on that as opposed to, say, just cutting the trees down and letting private or forest service people exploit them for timber? In other words, how do you put quantified values on this to make a semi-rational decision?

MR. POWELL: I agree with you about the large quantum of irrationality in many of the topmost public decisions. I am sure you are right in saying that we misrepresent what really happens when we say the government has decided this, the government has decided that, as though they had started with a clean sheet, had all the factors arranged and came to a balanced decision. Usually the decision will be far prejudiced one way or the other before it appears publicly to be taken.

I do not take it that this invalidates the big distinction which I was seeking to draw between the fact that all public decisions, however arrived at, whether rational or prejudiced, are by their nature specific and by their nature preemptive and are thus in fundamental contrast with decisions (if I may use the same word) arrived at through the market process.

For example, you said, and I am sure rightly, that a government decision to manufacture a particular weapon or to have it manufactured by a particular firm is often a decision largely forced upon the decision makers. But (to take that particular case) in a market situation—if sovereignty were not in play—there would be no question of the aircraft being made at all if it didn't pay. There would be no question of the aircraft being made by one firm if another firm could make it more efficiently.

So we still have, I think, this fundamental cleavage between the specificity of government decisions, i.e., unitary decisions, and the generality of the decisions arrived at automatically through the market system.

On your second point, I would say that when, in the case you pose, the nation says, "Let's have a national park, let us preserve an area of wild America as it was when the first settlers came," this is just like the decision to put a man on the moon or the decision to defend one's national existence. It is one which is deliberately taken as incommensurable.

Let me test it this way. Supposing a voice from heaven told Congress when it was passing wilderness legislation, "Listen, Congress, if you don't pass this bill, the United States will be richer, you will be better off if you don't preserve the wilderness." The answer, I imagine, which Congress would give is, "Thank you for nothing. We happen not to be interested in making that comparison. We have decided upon this for its own sake and we are treating it as an incommensurable."

The money calculus is only useful where people are

anyhow prepared to make comparisons and to be guided by comparisons, *in money terms.* I think the instance you gave is a typical instance of a unitary decision which is taken with an incommensurable object.

HERBERT STEIN, Brookings Institution: I would like to follow up on what you have just said about incommensurability because it seems to me that there are very few decisions that in fact we do make this way.

While Congress does not hear a voice from on high telling it where a limit might be, it does hear a voice from the taxpayer back home which does set limits to these things. I think we have gotten over our first flush of enthusiasm about putting a man on the moon and are becoming aware of many of the things that we would privately prefer to have. We are, you may have noticed in our papers, having a kind of taxpayers' revolt in this country.

I think that we do get an expression of the valuation that people put on their private uses of their income through their resistance to the payment of taxes for these functions which, of course, people talk about as if they were absolute goods but which we always do within some limits.

But I think there is a point in this wilderness example which is more general and I would like to hear you comment on that. It seems to me that the big push in this country now for the expansion of specific government action arises from what economists for a long time have called externalities. That is, we are very conscious of the fact that we are all living crowded together and that everything anybody does affects everybody else. We have aspects of it, like water pollution, air pollution, congestion of the streets, and so on.

This looks like the big field, the big new justification for expansion of direct government controls. I wonder if you have any comments on the extent to which this is, say, a legitimate case, whether there is some logical defect in this kind of case?

MR. POWELL: On your first point, I entirely agree that these decisions of government, though apparently absolute in character—e.g., "let us have a wilderness"— are in practice limited because clearly one wouldn't decree that 49 of the 50 states should be preserved as wilderness. But the limit in such decisions is a limit arbitrarily arrived at as a result of pressures and counter-pressures of a different kind from those which produce the allocation of resources under a market system.

There will surely in all such cases be an element of deliberate neglect of measurable economic advantage. In other words, although clearly one would stop short, very far short of 49 wildnerness states out of 50, one might well be prepared to take hundreds of thousands of acres—the amount is arbitrary—which could have yielded a high economic return, and for the sake of the incommensurable values which, as a community, we plump for having, preserve them as a wilderness. To parody Tacitus, we "make a wilderness and call it bliss."

Now as to your second point, certainly we commonly

use in Britain the words "social cost." It is the same point. With us as with you, the argument for the extension of specific government decision is often spearheaded by propositions about social costs.

My own view is that the social consequences of decisions taken through the market mechanism can be adequately safeguarded by general prescriptions and prohibitions which leave the market and choice free to operate within them.

You mentioned, for instance, pollution of the air and water. Well, avoidance of pollution of the air can be dealt with by prohibition. One can say: nobody shall emit x, y, z; but one does not need to produce the result of clear air by taking over all the factories and managing them in such a way that they emit no smoke.

Thus, social consequences can be taken care of, to a large extent, by prohibition, by the regulative action of the community, the framework of law, as I called it in my paper, which enables the mechanism of choice through the market and of allocation of tasks and resources through the market to function, subject only to that outside limitation.

I would add that I have never really seen a convincing demonstration of social costs which can be measured and which yet cannot be dealt with by the negative, prohibitory method.

For example, there is the case often urged in Britain —and I imagine it is urged here—that when a manufacturer decides to move in or to start up in an area where there is already a great amount of manufacture, he imposes on all the rest who are there social costs which may not for him be prohibitive but which may be so for others.

It seems to me that this argument—or at any rate the implicit argument, that therefore there should be a regulation which permits so many additional factories to be built but not more than that—overlooks the fact that the margin is constantly moving around. Maybe for manufacturer A, who moves into London, the social costs which he causes are not such as to deter him and not such as to make it not worth his while to start up his process in that place. But somewhere at the margin there will be somebody else for whom the congestion, rising labor costs, all sorts of other rising costs, of power, facilities, etc., will make his operations no longer economic in that area, so that he has to move. In the end a better economic use of resources has been produced.

So it seems to me that the market system is in fact taking care of that sort of comparison quite adequately, though not predictably. People are confusing the fact that they cannot identify how the market takes account of externalities with the proposition that the market does *not* take account of externalities. I believe in reality it does, though you can't identify the ways in which it does so or the places at which it does so.

HOLMES ALEXANDER, McNaught Syndicate: I would like to zero in on the ideological. We have a reference point here, and it is going to be difficult for you to answer, I am sure, but by preachment and satire an awful lot of philosophers down through the ages have built ideal governments. I mean Christ did it and Samuel Butler did it, the Greeks, and many others.

Now, I wondered if you could tell us what your concept of—I won't say an ideal republic is, because that would offend your Monarch in England—an ideal democracy or an ideal government would be so that we can take off from there. Is that too broad? I don't think it is.

MR. POWELL: I don't know whether you will be able to take off from my launching pad. And I must confess that I find the collocation of Christ and Samuel Butler more complimentary to the latter than to the former.

MR. ALEXANDER: He was their god, you know, and had many ideas of punishment. Disease instead of crime and, you know, all that complication.

MR. POWELL: I find the invitation to sketch out my ideal democracy a very, if you will pardon my saying so, American question. And it's a very American question addressed to a very English Englishman. (You can be an Englishman even though you are Welsh.)

The question isn't one to which I can attach any sort of meaning. It is not one which I pose to myself. It is not one to which an implied or explicit answer is necessary to me in a lifetime as a politician.

I am only politically self-conscious in a particular society, in this particular political society, namely, that of Britain. So far as I have ideals, which is an inappropriate word—I prefer to say political objects—they are much more concerned with the removal of blemishes or the avoidance of dangers than with the assimilation of the British Constitution to a platonic idea of a democracy which pre-exists in the mind.

I find myself much more in the position of either the agriculturist or the physician in the presence of an organic thing exposed to certain dangers, to certain diseases, and to certain deteriorations, who does his best with his limited knowledge and skill, to cure or to avert.

Now, I have attempted to describe the sort of frame of mind in which I think most, in which certainly all Tory British politicians approach their task. They do not start from a notion of democracy and then say, "Whoopee, aren't we lucky we live in a democracy too?" and then go on to say, "How do we make this even nearer to the perfect democracy?"

On the contrary, they say, "How interesting that we have been born into this society which, by a sort of circularity of reasoning, we find approvable and satisfying. Have we any worries about it? Have we any anxieties about it? Are there any changes in it taking place more or less of their own accord which could perhaps be canalized or guided or formalized or diverted?" This is much more the frame of mind of the political society from which I come.

I don't know whether that's enough to take off from.

WILLIAM G. COLMAN, Commission on Intergovernmental Relations: Would you agree that the processes

of research and development as they evolve in a free
market system cause in turn an inescapable increase in
the absolute number of specific decisions that government has to make, not necessarily an increase in the
relative number but an increase in the absolute number?

MR. POWELL: I don't see why the area of specific
government decision should be larger in a highly developed technological age or society than in a very primitive one. In fact, it seems to me a thesis could be made
that in a primitive society the specific area of government is likely to be, and may even need—for the survival of the society—to be, larger than in one more—
may I use the word? We haven't had it this evening so
far—sophisticated.

I don't know if I have answered your question at all.
Perhaps I misunderstood it.

MR. COLMAN: No, you understood it. I would
use this example. I think there are many others. Twenty
years ago we did not have television. Today we have it.
Channels have to be regulated by government and assigned by government. Now, maybe they don't have
to be assigned by government.

MR. POWELL: No. They only have to be assigned by
government insofar as public and common interests
are involved.

Now, if the government, for defense purposes, wanted
a whole band of frequencies, then, of course, it would
say, "These frequencies are forbidden to everyone else,"
as we do with the police. It wouldn't have to go on and

say, "And of the rest we will allocate bands all around
this table."

JOHN MIDGELY, *The Economist* of London: Could
I take it a bit further on that? We had rather a curious
spectacle in Britain, or that is on the fringe of Britain,
in the last few years in which gangs of radio program
operators were seizing points of vantage off the coast,
including former defense installations and so on, and
operating them for profit. There were occasions in which
one gang would board an installation and expel another.

Now, these are not questions of specific government
needs of things but wouldn't the government inherently
have to guard itself against the approach of chaos in that
sort of thing?

MR. POWELL: First, insofar as one citizen commits
a violent act against another, clearly this is within the
scope of the administration of law and order, which
must be unitary and must be a matter of common administration and decision. I have clearly set this out in
my paper.

Secondly, there are equally clearly involved in the use
of radio frequencies, considerations of public safety, such
as safety of shipping, and I have mentioned the possibility
of bands being required for defense and for police purposes. Here again, quite clearly it is implicit in the very
nature of an organized community that a specific decision is taken to earmark that facility or part of a facility.

But thirdly it does not seem to me to be necessary that
from that you go on and say that allocation of what

remains should take place arbitrarily and not through the market. The market is prefectly capable of allocating the unoccupied area which the state has not appropriated to itself for its own purposes.

WILLIAM COPENHAVER, House Government Operations Committee: Mr. Powell, I would like to pose a question to you in sort of a follow-up to the one Mr. Alexander posed, if I may, seeking to base it on what I grasped to be your statement and your philosophy contained in it. If I am wrong, I am subject to correction.

If I follow what you said, in general terms, the size of government in one country may be or is determined by the competitive instincts vis-à-vis the second country, the country-versus-country thesis. If this were true, then the type of philosophy underlying the type of government established would be secondary or even inconsequential to the overall proposition.

Is it not a fact that the type of philosophy of a government frequently determines the degree of competitiveness within the country and thereby creates a wavelike effect upon the philosophy of other countries? Thus, is it not the case that the philosophy of government is the ultimate control?

But in most forms of life, doesn't stagnation set in under one system and thereby tend to force a new system to be developed which in turn creates a wavelike effect throughout the world? If different philosophies may breed different sizes of formal government, laissez faire, anarchy, theocracy, and what-have-you, and, if you basically are dissatisfied with the size of the government, the formal government that you are faced with now because of a different philosophy, you may seek to institute deliberate actions to create a different form, i.e., a marketplace economy or a central form of government. But perhaps you will actually in the long run have to wait for the existing government to run its course, for this existing philosophy to run its course, before a second form can come back in. It may not be going from one to another and to another on a continuum but back and forth?

Perhaps your theory is 30 or 40 years in the scenes, although you, as a leader in your country, are seeking to put forward this philosophy in the hope that it will catch on and in the hope that your country will adopt it. This will thereby create a more vibrant economy which will create a wavelike effect in other nations to adopt it, just as the Eastern European and Soviet economies have found that maybe they can be more wealthy and create greater competition by going over to more of a marketplace economy. And this may actually have the effect of swinging us eventually farther toward a marketplace economy?

MR. POWELL: I am prepared to accept that the fact of my putting forward a personal opinion—indeed, of a large group of people putting forward a personal opinion and preference—doesn't bring with it necessarily or predictably any alteration in the form of the society to which we belong.

Indeed, I meant that, when in an early sentence of my paper I described those of us who today offer our own answer to the question as borne on the tides and currents. I went on to say that we are indicators of their direction, but we may well be indicating a side eddy and not the main current as it will appear when viewed in hindsight from some future date.

So I am entirely with you in your implication that there isn't a straightforward development or sequence in the changing forms of society and that the mere fact that arguments are put forward even with compelling force doesn't necessarily produce corresponding changes in the society to which they are addressed. To that extent, I agree entirely with what you said.

Secondly—I think you must be right in saying that there is some overspill from one society to another, that there is an influence which one society can objectively be observed to have upon another, either because it demonstrates physically that it is superior or because it looks superior to those who examine it from the outside. So I think I must agree with you that there is bound to be an interaction between societies which may partly explain some of the historical movements in this direction or that, which with hindsight we observe.

Where I wasn't sure we were in agreement was the setting in which I had placed the competitive instinct in my paper. The context in which I referred to it was that wherever we find government taking specific decisions these decisions are being taken once for the community as a whole. In other words, the community in all such cases is acting, however figuratively, as an individual. Now, that individual—that nation individual or that society individual—sees itself in a context, it sees itself introspectively but it also sees itself, as human individuals do, in the context of the outside world. This is why, when these specific unitary decisions of government are in play, we can usually observe that the society which takes them is comparing itself consciously, is conscious of how it is getting on in comparison with other countries. I exemplified this with the league tables of "growth" and with competition in lunar research. We could find it, I think, in very many of the fields of specific government decision, i.e., decision taken once and for all on behalf of all the members of the community.

It is only that point—the sense in which I was using competition and emulation in my paper—where I wasn't sure that you were with me.

HARVEY SEGAL, *Washington Post*: What you described with your concept of incommensurability and your league table of nations is a revival of the spirit of mercantilism. If that is true, how do you account for this development?

MR. POWELL: I don't understand in what sense my reference to incommensurability was a revival of the spirit of mercantilism. If you could, perhaps you would help me a little.

MR. SEGAL: In the mercantilist period, first of all,

there were literally the league tables of nations. I am thinking of Gregory Keating who was a pioneer national income accountant who actually ranked the rate of population growth—England, France, the Netherlands, and the like—and would be very much concerned if England's population growth rate was falling behind. The colony, the colonial impulse with your prestige drive or your drive toward emulation—I could go on——

MR. POWELL: Yes, I see.

MR. SEGAL:—with undeclared war and the like.

MR. POWELL: I see, thank you very much. If you are saying that economic growth set as an object and defined as an object by government and so defined in a spirit of competition, is retrogressive—is, as I think I said somewhere, harking back two centuries—I agree with you very much.

MR. SEGAL: What I want to know is: How do you account for the revival of this spirit at this juncture in history?

MR. POWELL: Oh, that's more difficult, isn't it? It's one thing to think you identify a change which is taking place and quite another to seek to account for it. No, I am sorry. I am either too little or too much of a historian to venture upon an answer to that.

MR. MIDGELY: Hasn't there been a transference of the emulative spirit from other symbols of national importance to this symbol at a time when external military power and so on has been more or less denied?

MR. POWELL: I think that is certainly so of Britain.

Some of our malaise today in Britain, our national flagellation, is that we seek some solace for what we regard as the loss of power and empire and so on and think perhaps that this might be found in terms of economic achievement. Then we are dismayed when the indices of ecoonmic achievement served up by OEEC or the United Nations, or whoever it may be, persistently show us in the wrong part of the table.

I am not sure whether this is a general answer to the question asked just before, but I am certain you are right, sir, in saying that it has a relevance to Britain's present psychological predicament.

NORMAN TURE, National Bureau of Economic Research: Mr. Powell, I am sure that everyone in this room found your remarks extremely provocative because we are all searching for, I think, some clues that will help us to distinguish between the activity that is proper for the private sector and that for the public sector.

Therefore, we respond, I think, very positively to any suggestions of such distinctions. But I would suggest that perhaps they have been just a shade overstated. When I think of a distinction that you have drawn between the decision-making process in the public sector—and in the whole, you know, the confluence of activity that surrounds that decision—and in the private sector, those distinctions do not strike me as very sharp.

That is to say I think I see in the private sector the same sort of prematurity in decision making that you attribute to the public sector. I think I see the same tendency to invest a highly specific character in the kind of activity that a particular business concern wants to undertake. As for the attributions of incommensurability, my heavens, every major business concern in the United States is at pains to convince all who will listen— and those who can't help but listen—that their products are completely differentiated from those of all possible rivals and that there is some unique virtue in their consumption.

MR. POWELL: But do they convince them?

MR. TURE: Well, the distinction is: if they find that they are not at the present moment in fact succeeding in being persuasive, then they invest some additional resources in advertising. This is the distinction that I think I have made. They are, at the time that they make that additional investment in advertising, prepared, however reluctantly or unhappily, to concede the possibility of a failure of the advertising campaign; whereas, the government, when it finds that it has not been adequately persuasive, adduces some additional advertising with the complete conviction that there is no possible question about the outcome.

So, you know, I don't really find these formulations operationally useful in trying to tell me the answers to the kind of question I think is very pressing in the United States today. In the setting that we now live in, short of revolution, we would like to find some way of making the public decision-making process better than it now is. We would like to have some mechanisms or systems that would give us greater assurance than we now have that what the public sector does through time will be more useful than it now is.

So it seems to me that perhaps maybe some clues might be found, and perhaps you would address yourself to this question. Maybe the clues are to be found in the genesis of decision making in the public sector as opposed to the private sector.

MR. POWELL: That is a very interesting field you have opened to me. I am sure it is a persistent ambition of mankind to make its kings better. You will remember Plato looked forward to the time when philosophers would be kings and Bernard Shaw looked forward to the time—which is more sympathetic to me—when professors of Greek would be politicians. I am afraid, as a functioning politician, the best advice I can give to those who look to an improvement in their rulers is to keep as much as they can out of their rulers' hands. That is the most practical method of keeping the ruler from making a mess of things. I would hope for more success from removing spheres of decision from government than from improving government. I am only giving you some of the working rules of thumb of a workaday politician, but it is a general rule of thumb in politics that, for political purposes, human nature is constant. If you find a politician saying his policies are all right, only the trouble is that the people aren't good enough or that he looks to an improvement of the human species which will make his policies workable or that people have got to learn or be taught to do this and that, you may be sure you are in the presence of a very bad politician.

I believe that the weaknesses of government are much the same from age to age and that they are founded in the unchanging characteristics of human nature, individually and collectively. Therefore, for what it is worth, I would counsel you against devoting any time or energy to attempting to improve government.

While I would accept that I have been attempting a descriptive task in what I have said, I have not been attempting a normative task. In nothing that I have said do I believe there can be any basis of judgment, anything which would help the people of these States to decide whether to entrust to this or that sector public authority. I am afraid my paper is innocent of a basis for any such deduction.

In your criticism of my description, however, I do think you raised what, with respect, I take for a confusion and a very common one. When I criticize government economic planning, the commonest, almost invariable thing is that somebody will get up at the back of the hall, when it comes to questions and say: "But is it not a fact that when Mr. Powell was Minister of Health he produced a plan for a hospital service?" [Laughter.] This is supposed to be a refutation of what I had said about the weaknesses and disadvantages of government economic planning.

Now, the argument is not about whether to plan or not, any more than about whether to think or not; it is about who should think about what and who should plan what. Of course, the individual plans, the firm plans, and they incur all the same penalties a government incurs when taking a specific decision—the penalties of prematurity, imperfect information, mixed motives, and so on. But when we refer to the allocation of resources and the identification of tasks by the market, we are not referring to the partially frustrated and partially fulfilled plans of individuals and firms, but to the outcome of their interaction.

May I take the crude case which I gave to illustrate this—North Sea gas? In order to produce a plan, a national economic plan, for 1970 in 1960, one had to assume, in fact one did assume—and, given the particular period, it would be true to say that one had to assume—that there was no such thing as North Sea gas.

Now in 1960 almost everybody else was assuming that there was no such thing as North Sea gas. The important thing, however, is that there were some people who were assuming that there might well be such a thing as North Sea gas. And, as soon as they began to turn out to be right, all the other plans and intentions which were continuously being formed by firms and individuals were modified *ambulando*.

That is not the process which takes place when the state says, "This is going to be the pattern of the economy in 1970." When the state says this, it says so with the voice of sovereignty. It says, "We have decided, on behalf of all of you, that this is how it will be in 1970 and, by God, we'll make it so, if we can." Whether they do so by force or whether they pretend they are doing so by persuasion, the principle is the same.

Thus, although a government in planning and an individual in planning are going through the same mental processes, the effect of a government taking a specific economic decision and of hundreds of thousands of individuals continuously taking specific economic decisions for themselves, are different in kind. It is that distinction which I sought to make.

RODNEY CROWTHER, *Baltimore Sun:* When the government finally gets down to the place where everybody believes or a majority of the people believe that it should be the decision maker and it successively and continuously makes decisions which begin to run things into the ground, what course have the people got but to overthrow the government?

MR. POWELL: This I would have thought must depend upon the particular constitution you are working under. In some countries shooting is the method. In others it's done by various more subtle methods. I cannot see, with respect, sir, and I am not trying to evade the question, that there can be any general answer.

If you like, the opportunity for citizens, unrebuked, to draw attention earlier rather than later to the fact that the direction is groundward is presumably conducive to the survival of the society in which that is possible. That is one of the grounds on which one would argue for the survivability of societies such as those to which we both belong, which accept maximum free discussion as a desirable thing.

I think this is the only general proposition that I can offer in reply.

RONALD STONE, Staff Assistant to the Secretary for the Majority, United States Senate: We heard last week that it is a warfare world and not the welfare state that causes big government. I think a perfect example might be—maybe the best example might be— as C. Northcote Parkinson points out in the case of the Royal Navy: for every man in the Navy at sea there are ten in administration. So this is question Number One: Isn't improvement from within perhaps the only possible solution?

And, secondly, knowing your interest in the Far East, how might we lower the basic demands for these expenditures?

MR. POWELL: As a matter of fact, in Britain defense expenditure is only about one-quarter or one-fifth of total central government expenditure in the budget—"above and below the line" (I know we don't have the "line" now, but it's still a valid distinction of importance)—running at some nine-thousand-million. The defense budget is around two-thousand-million. So it wouldn't be true of Britain to say, even of central government expenditure, that defense is the lion's share. If we were to add in, as we properly should, public expenditure by subordinate authorities or statutory public authorities, we should find the fraction much smaller. So I find the starting point unconvincing.

It may well be that in a federal country one sees these things differently because, of course, when you look at a federal budget, if the federal functions are largely defense, then you will see a much higher proportion of federal expenditure in defense. This happens, I am sure, in any federal country. It happens in the German *Bund* as opposed to *Land* budgets. But, if you put them all together, as you should—we are a unitary state in Britain—then I don't think in either of our two countries you would find that defense expenditure is anything like the lion's share of public expenditure.

I am afraid I have to say the same about the Far East. Speaking only as I must for Britain—or rather "of" Britain, for I have no authority to speak "for" Britain— our expenditure in the Far East, assuming that one is going to keep approximately the same forces under arms anyhow, is negligible, relatively negligible in budgetary terms. Expenditure measured in terms of foreign exchange is less negligible, but then that takes us into the question of whether one is wise to measure expenditure in terms of foreign exchange rather than in terms of real resources in whatever currency expressed.

So it wouldn't be true at any rate of the British defense budget to say that in claims upon real resources the Far East as a sector, as a theater, represented more than a small fraction of our defensive effort.

JAMES STEINER, National Chamber of Commerce: As a quick preamble to a question, in the decision-making process which you have spoken of, when the alternatives are not measured objectively because some alternatives are made as you have said incommensurable with other alternatives, can we, after one or two or three decades, after these decisions have been made in the past, of course, then reflect and go back and attempt to conduct an objective evaluation of government programs?

A proposal of this kind is in existence here. So my questions are two:

Has there been an evaluation by Parliament of some of the long-standing British programs which constitute major spending activities? If there has been or if there hasn't been, what would you recommend be the specific elements for examination to make a meaningful comparison for the purposes of evaluation, giving priorities to these programs so that we can sort out the essential from the nonessential, and with the emotions generated by the political conditions at time of passage removed by two or three decades? Is there something specific that we can compare?

MR. POWELL: Alas, I think this is a vain aspiration. I don't believe you can have an objective evaluation of the effect of a past program, if that was directed to incommensurable ends.

Let's take the British National Health Service and let's go on a couple of decades. What are we asking ourselves in the 1980s about the National Health Service in the 1950s? Are we asking ourselves whether the population would have been more healthy in its absence? How on earth do we set about answering that question?

We cannot know by definition in what directions the resources compulsorily directed to that pattern of medical care would otherwise have been applied. We cannot know and I do not know how we set about forming a notion, whether, as in the United States, there would in fact have been more medical care, though a different bundle, or whether more would have been spent instead upon candies to rot the teeth and tobacco to damage hearts and lungs.

It simply isn't possible to evaluate, to compare, what you have decided not to compare. In setting out to have a National Health Service, you have decided to prevent people from comparing results, from making the choice between that application and some other application of the thousand-million pounds which the National Health Service costs. That is what it is intended to do, to prevent people making the choice; so you can't job backwards in 30 years' time and say, "If they had not been denied the choice, this is the pattern on which they would have exercised it."

Even if you could do that, even if some research foundation in the year 1980 could say, "Had there not been a National Health Service in the 1950s, the following is a description of what would have been the British economy from 1950 to 1960," how do you then set about deciding which would have been preferable?

I am afraid you are back to these crude political preferences. *Des Menschen Wille ist sein Himmelreich,* as Goethe says: "What a man wants is for him the kingdom of heaven." 'Tis so of a nation.

CARL A. S. COAN, Housing Subcommittee of the Senate Committee on Banking and Currency: I may be duplicating or may be raising some of the same questions that have been raised earlier but, if you will bear with me, I would like to explore this a little further with you. I am thinking of what Senator Douglas said last week when he ended up his meeting and said something like human values should be supreme values.

MR. POWELL: Which human values?

MR. COAN: Human values should be supreme values in making judgments on how big our government should be.

MR. POWELL: But which human values?

MR. COAN: I suppose these are decisions that somebody has to make, that we are talking about human values rather than material values now. I think you and he might have a good time next week describing what you mean by human values and maybe that can be pulled out. But I find in what you said several things.

One is that you state that a decision made in the nongovernment sector would be more meaningful, more productive. You imply that there will be many groups making this decision and by the fact that there will be many groups making the decision, the decision will be a better decision than if the government made it.

But are you taking into account perhaps big business? To the extent we have big business, maybe these decisions are not going to be as good as they would otherwise be. Isn't that almost like perhaps big government making the decision?

MR. POWELL: I've read Galbraith too.

MR. COAN: The other thing I think is the fact that when you do make these decisions, these are decisions which relate to the material things, and you seemed to me to say that the best government is the least government. . . .

MR. POWELL: No, I didn't.

MR. COAN: You did not say that?

MR. POWELL: No.

A VOICE: Maybe it was Barry Goldwater.

MR. COAN: I thought he and Barry Goldwater were using the same language on that score.

MR. POWELL: I don't know what language he uses.

MR. COAN: I got the impression that you believed that it is impossible to improve government and therefore I would assume it is your conclusion that the best government is the least government. Maybe you want to explain that a little.

MR. POWELL: Yes, certainly. Forgive me if I say— and it would really have been a poor evening if this had not happened—that over and over again when one is addressing adults one has the experience that they come with the knowledge of what one is going to say and depart with the knowledge that one has said it. This is one of the great advantages of addressing the top form in schools and the earlier years in the degree course. During the later years of a degree course I find that the "shades of the prison house begin to close" and students come to the lecture knowing what you are going to say and go away convinced that you have said it.

Now, I said very few in fact of the things that you have attributed to me. I haven't as yet had the pleasure and advantage of reading Senator Douglas' text, but I shall find myself entirely in agreement with him, if he says that if Leviathan, if the community, decides that this is its will, that it wants a wilderness or that it wants a National Health Service or that it wants a great navy, who is to argue with it? Who shall sit in judgment upon it? If so, he and I shall agree.

The only area in which I have allowed myself to compare, and then only in terms of efficiency, the specific decision of government and the result thrown up by market forces is the area where all are agreed, where there is general agreement—you will find those words in my text—that the criteria are economic values monetarily measurable.

It is only in that area—which may be large or small, according to taste, which cannot be objectively defined or normatively defined—that you can validly compare the result of specific government decision with market results.

Now, you say, perfectly correctly, that the market is never perfect and sometimes it is more imperfect than

at other times. To which I say, Amen. From that I de-
duce that in any society which is using the market as
the means of allocation of the tasks and effort of its
citizens, where economic criteria are accepted, endeavor
will be devoted towards rendering the market less imperfect: antitrust laws, anti-monopoly laws, anti-restrictive practices and so on. There have to be police in the
economic as well as the social fields of society.

I do think, however, that we tend to exaggerate the
imperfection produced by large economic units. This is
a rather tedious debate and I won't go into it at any
length, but it is a matter of common knowledge that
large economic units don't seem to have much more
success than smaller economic units in imposing their
will upon the consumer. They seem to be almost as
much at the prey of market forces.

But, even if that were not so, there would, I think,
be this important distinction—it was a distinction made
by Charles I shortly before his execution—between a
public monopoly, that is to say a government's specific
economic decision, and a private monopoly: the former
is a king and the second is a subject. As Charles I said,
"A king and a subject are two things." In other words,
you can bust a private monopoly with the state, but you
can't bust a state monopoly with the state; and this is
rather an important difference.

MR. ALEXANDER: Sir, during the recess you told
me in response to a question that you didn't achieve
your seat in your constituency by your personality,

which is considerable, or your arguments, which are forceful, but by a groundswell, a philosophical, ideological trend—

MR. POWELL: No, just a groundswell.

MR. ALEXANDER: I am hopeful that, from what you have said, this is the wave of the future. I just wish, if you would, if you could, that you would describe or designate that groundswell that lifted you to your seat, because I hope it will happen in many places.

MR. POWELL: Thank you very much. I don't think that the psephologists have got anywhere yet. I number several of them amongst my friends. I cooperate with them, you know, in what I regard as their vain investigations and experiments. No, experiments isn't the right word. That is just the trouble. This is a non-experimental science.

We have no means of comparing the behavior of an electorate, even at two successive elections, and, if you can't do that, there is jolly little you can find out about the *causes* of electoral behavior.

I notice one or two eyebrows raised, so let me explain. Let us take a constituency in which there is a majority of 2,000. (You see, we have much smaller constituencies and we also, in typical English fashion, think in small figures.) Where there is a majority of 2,000 at one election for party A and a majority of 2,000 for party B at the other election, "Uh-huh," says the psephologist, "you see, a floating vote of 2,000, so let's go and find the 2,000 who changed."

It is not so. At least, if it is so, it's a fluke. That result can be produced in an infinite number of ways. It can be produced by nobody changing his vote, if a sufficient number of people have died and become 21. That is entirely sufficient to produce a change from 2,000 one way to 2,000 the other within two or three years. But you can't investigate the people who have died and the people who have come onto the register, because you don't know how the people who are 21 and voting at the second election would have voted if they had been 21 and voting at the first election, and you don't know how the people in the cemetery would be voting now, if they weren't in the cemetery.

So it is absolutely hopeless, even on this extremely simple case, to imagine that you can discover even what has happened. And that is a very early stage towards discovering why it has happened. All we know, therefore, is that objectively we do discern a sort of, I used the word, "groundswell" and I will use it again—a very vague, generalized sort of wave movement. It cannot be terribly particular because the party forms into which it is cast, the channels, the sluices through which the swell flows and ebbs, are changing in shape all the time.

I mean, the Liberal is becoming a Scottish Nationalist and the Scottish Nationalist is becoming a Liberal and what does the psephologist do with that, I would like to know? Well, perhaps we shall learn after the by-election which is taking place today.

A VOICE: He lost.

MR. POWELL: Who lost?

SAME VOICE: Winston Churchill.

MR. POWELL: Aah, but Winston Churchill didn't have the advantage of being opposed by a Scottish Nationalist in the Gorton division of Manchester. No, no.

So we have this very general groundswell. What I do know about it is that it is absolutely terrifying in its uniformity, that the variation, whatever it is and whatever its causes are, in different places and in different constituencies, is frighteningly uniform.

THIRD SESSION

MR. POWELL: Like the Senator, I, with respect, found the presentation this evening less opaque than that of a fortnight before. Perhaps that is because in debate and personal confrontation, which is certainly an essential part of both our political systems, one gets to understand better the points of differences and the points of agreement. But it seemed to me as I listened to Senator Douglas that the term "Tory" conveyed to him all the overtones and undertones of 1775, historically correct or otherwise.

Now, to me, not unnaturally, Tory implies something very different. I would have said that one of the distinguishing characteristics of the British Tories is that we have always asserted the primacy of sovereignty acting on behalf of the community. We have been readier than any other party to assert that noneconomic aims and ends should override economic ends. We have been readier than any of our opponents to give primacy to the noneconomic ends.

There are a number of examples of that from recent history brought up by what Senator Douglas said. He was very complimentary about my personal record, as he called it, in attack on monopoly. But this is not a personal record. It so happens that in the last ten years a Conservative government in Britain passed the first effective British legislation against restrictive practices. That was Mr. Peter Thornycroft's Restrictive Practices Act of 1956. Mr. Heath in 1964 passed an act under which resale price maintenance has virtually disappeared already.

So that it is really impossible to assert that the Conservative party in Britain has not shown itself in principle ready and even eager to introduce the legislation which will improve and police competition.

Then again, on the question of social costs as evinced by air pollution and pollution of water and so on, it so happens that I myself, as Parliamentary Secretary to the Ministry of Housing and Local Government in 1956, had the honor of carrying through our Parliament our first clean air act. Under this law, the prohibitive and regulative powers of the state were used to say to all and sundry: Engage in what industrial processes you please but, in doing so, there are certain rules which you must observe and these will be policed in the following way. We were not afraid, not reluctant, to extend the clean air inspectorate for that purpose. This is an activity of government which seems to me wholly within the philosophy of the Conservative party.

And what is the alternative? Those who make much of social costs in this debate of "How Big Should Government Be?" seem to be implying that social costs can only be taken account of by positive action—that is to say, only if a community itself undertakes the economic activities and does this thing here and that thing there or refrains from this or that economic activity. My submission is that the social costs which are capable of being identified can be taken care of, if you so decide, by general regulatory prohibitive action which does not interfere with, but sets the framework for, the activity of the market.

The biggest misunderstanding between us seems to be in the area of redistribution. Might I take the case, which the Senator mentioned, of the widow's pension.

Now, there is much in the history of the Conservative party in Britain which shows that we have been very ready to use the power of the state redistributively to guarantee to every member of the community what is generally felt to be a standard of living below which no one should fall. I would assert that that principle is as good Tory as any other. But let us follow this through a little. The state redistributes by using its sovereign power to earmark a quantum of resources and to redistribute it and so, by redistributing it, to increase the purchasing power of certain individuals or classes who are identified. This is a very different approach from seeking the same end by interfering with the price mechanism and the market.

Let me stay on the pension. One of the things which I am happiest to look back on in my own legislative record is that it fell to me as Financial Secretary in 1957 to abolish the tobacco concessions. We had this pernicious institution whereby an old-age pensioner could obtain tobacco at a concessionary price. It led to all sorts of dishonesty and malpractices and in my view was a degrading as well as an inefficient approach to the object in view. For example, it favored the pensioner who happened to be a tobacco smoker as against the pensioner who happened to prefer to lay out his or her income in some other way. That's a minor example but we have major examples.

In the field of housing, we select recipients and cheapen the article, in order to benefit them, thus damaging the price mechanism. We have suffered for 50 years in Britain from the attempt to assist, by destroying the price mechanism in rented housing, those whom we say are unable to afford a decent standard of housing. The approach which respects and uses the market, and I couldn't have paid it a more fulsome eulogium than the Senator did—

SENATOR DOUGLAS: I wanted to strengthen your argument.

MR. POWELL: I am much obliged, sir. I am accepting your assistance with gratitude, Senator. The approach which preserves all of the advantages of the market and still achieves the noneconomic ends of the community is the redistributive approach that says: decide what level of purchasing power the community as a whole wishes to attribute to a particular group, and then give them that purchasing power calculated at the market rate. Don't give them a bundle of concessionary things, concessionary coal, concessionary housing, concessionary tobacco. Give them what you consider is the appropriate purchasing power and let them be self-respecting members of the community with the same freedom and choice in laying that out as anyone else has in laying out their income.

So I think the Senator and I share to a very great extent the view that there is an undeniable function of a redistributive character for the government in any community. I would hope that we could join together in demanding that that redistributive function be done openly and honestly by the supplementation or provision of purchasing power and not covertly and dishonestly by fudging the prices of some of the requirements of the beneficiaries and thus destroying the benefits which, as he himself glowingly illustrated, the market mechanism can provide.

At this stage, I would like to go no further. I have made my bid towards a reconciliation between the Quaker and the High Anglican, between the Rebel and the Loyalist of 1775 and between the friends and allies on one side of the Atlantic and the other.

SENATOR DOUGLAS: I appreciate this discussion because it indicates more and more how our good friend is moving to agree with us liberal members of the Democratic party. If he were to stay here long enough, we might well count him as one of us.

I am afraid that when he lays down his slogan that the principle of the Tory party is to give sovereign action on behalf of the community that he will disappoint many of those who have brought him to this country. I anticipated the licking of chops which people would have at the thought of your coming here to slaughter the idea of community action and, lo and behold, you really agree that there should be community action to effect a redistribution of the fruits of income at least.

I am very glad that you mentioned the question of children's allowances, which I think is an excellent way. Without wishing again to heap undue credit upon myself, I think I was the first man in this country, over 40 years ago, to advocate children's allowances along with Miss Eleanor Rathbone, of your country, and others. I hope, therefore, that we can count you as a defender of this principle.

We don't wish to misquote you. We understand you do favor children's allowances. We will put this to very good use. Indeed, we have put the statements of Winston Churchill to very good use when we were carrying out our campaign for social security.

I was a little surprised that you made the Tory party the great advocate of social legislation. It is true that during the Victorian Period they did not have the same inhibitions against governmental action that the party of Bright and Cobden did. But there has since been an amalgamation of economic classes, of course, in Great Britain. The Tory party has ceased to be the landed party and the Liberal party the manufacturing or trading party. The two groups—the owning party, more or less—have come together as compared to the non-owners. That is the basic division in English political life. You can choose your party perhaps somewhat on that basis.

As I remember, in 1911, when I was a young man, the opposition to the social legislation of Lloyd George and Churchill, and Churchill was then, of course, a Liberal, a social reform Liberal, not a laissez-faire Liberal, the opposition to all this from the Conservative or Tory party was very intense indeed. It may be that with the growth of the Labor party, the Conservative party felt that it had to trim just so much in order to avoid complete extinction. I have detected certain tendencies in this direction amongst the Republicans of this country, that under the drubbing which they have received for the last third of a century they have become noticeably more compassionate and more humane in attitude than they were. This is really one of the great advantages of democracy, that you can melt the hardest hearts and transform them into people who really work for the benefit of the community.

Now, let me come back to the general thesis. We would be making a great mistake if we tried to deprecate the role of market price, a great mistake. But we sim-

ilarly would be making an equally great mistake if we
made it the sole arbiter of our values or even, in many
instances, the predominant arbiter of values because of
the inequalities in the present distribution of income,
because of the difference between individual cost and
social cost, the differences between many of the competitive weaknesses. I think the competitive features
of economic life are not always spiritually the best.
I hope that Mr. Powell's coming may moderate the
intensity with which those of you who wish to uphold
the market as the predominant guide in all circumstances may have your faith reduced. We will claim
him as a temporarily erring brother.

DR. C. LOWELL HARRISS, Columbia University:
Senator Douglas, why do people, do you believe, act
better, more humanely, more wisely through the political process than through the market process? I will
give you an example of the kind of thing I have in mind.
You have been concerned recently with the problems of
slums and urban ills. I would say that probably one of the
contributors to them has been the property tax, which
is an old institution, but not one of the glories of
mankind.

SENATOR DOUGLAS: I agree with you.

DR. HARRISS: Now, this is a political thing.

SENATOR DOUGLAS: I think that one of the
chief weaknesses of market prices flows out of the inequality of incomes. I happen to be one who believes
that this present inequality of incomes is ethically wrong.

There is no such inequality in the political field. A poor man has potentially the same voice as a rich man. In practice, of course, this is not so. He does not have the resources or the organization to carry out propaganda. But there is always the possibility that he may take offense if legislation either perpetuates or intensifies the inequality of incomes.

The equality at the ballot box, therefore, helps to offset the inequality in the marketplace and, as one who believes in a greater degree of equality in society, therefore, it seems to me that the ballot box can correct or partially correct the inequities. We have seen that work out.

Now, this does not work perfectly. It requires knowledge and knowledge is not freely available to the poor. It requires organization and organization is difficult for the poor to effect. But there is always the possibility that democracy might work and it does work to a limited extent. Hence it, to repeat, serves to modify and to improve the faulty distribution of the good things of life affected by sheer economic power.

DR. MILTON FRIEDMAN, University of Chicago: Senator Douglas, I am a little surprised by your answer just now. I would like to continue the discussion along this same line because I can well understand that in the abstract and in advance one might suppose that the political process would correct inequalities in the market —or at least help to correct them.

But it seems to me that in fact it has the quite

opposite effect. As I have observed the political process, the major reason why I am opposed to governmental action is because it seems to me that in case after case it strengthens the inequality that exists, that is, it widens the difference between the poor and the well-to-do. We have cases, of which we are all well aware, like percentage depletion, tariffs and quotas, and loopholes in the income tax. Every time there is a regulatory body like the ICC, this strengthens monopolies at the expense of competition.

The question I would like to put to you is whether in fact your comparison doesn't imply a double standard. On the one hand, you look at the imperfect market and we would all agree that it has many, many imperfections. You stress the imperfections and take them as of the essence of the market. On the other hand, you look at the political process—and we would agree that it has many imperfections—but, in that case, you take those as deviations from the true workings of the political process.

I would be one to question whether and how you would explain the fact that time and again the political process leads to policies which have the effect of hurting those people you and I would want to help and helping those people whom we would not want to hurt but at least we wouldn't want to help at the expense of the others.

Is that an accident?

SENATOR DOUGLAS: No, it is not an accident

but it results from a perversion of the democratic process. I hope you will forgive me for a personal reference. Nearly everything that you mention is an abuse that I have tried—

DR. FRIEDMAN: Oh, I know. I realize that. That is why I mentioned it.

SENATOR DOUGLAS: —to work against and I can tell you where our opposition came from. It came from the very people who thought or said that they were advocates of "free enterprise," but, in reality, were defenders of a special privilege. As a practical matter, when they chose up sides, the people who would try to reduce privilege were those who would be condemned as opponents of free enterprise. But I think they weren't.

I think there was a complete perversion of discussion and of real values in the debate. The forces of special privilege resent any effort to diminish their special privilege, resent any effort of government to protect the weak. All too often they are victorious, but this is not the fault of democracy. It is the fault of the unequal economic power which carries itself over into political discussions.

Take, for instance, this question of the depletion allowance. That involves billions of dollars. Those billions of dollars are powerfully organized, not only politically but economically as well, from the standpoint of newspapers, magazines, lobbyists, lawyers, public relations men, while the interests of the people are diffused, fragmented, weak. But nevertheless there is always the possibility that people may be informed and may wake up. At times they do, and this furnishes a directive.

If it had not been for the people having the vote, we would not have had free public education. That came in with Jacksonian democracy. The battle for this in England was fought over the opposition of Mr. Powell's party. If it had not been for popular democracy, we would not have had the development of public health. If it had not been for political democracy we would not have had pure foods and drugs.

I know something about the continuing battle on foods and drugs, because I was very close to my dear friend [the late Senator] Estes Kefauver. There is always the possibility of a popular revolt which enabled us to get some of this legislation through.

So I would say the trouble with legislation is not the presence of democracy but that of there not being sufficient democracy operating in the political field. A more informed public, a more alert public, a public with better representatives—and we all have these human weaknesses—would eliminate many of these things.

And I think about you, Milton, as I do about our friend Powell here, you really belong on our side much of the time, instead of taking pot shots at us.

DR. FRIEDMAN: That's the way I feel about you too, Paul.

MR. POWELL: We are all in manifest danger of ending up on the Senator's side—so persuasive is he.

I wonder if we have not slipped somewhat into altering the subject of the debate, which is "How Big Should Government Be?" and equating government, perhaps American-wise, with democracy. The Senator referred just now to food and drugs legislation. You can have food and drugs legislation enforced just as much by an autocratic government as by a democratic government. Perhaps we ought to keep the form of government and the sphere of government separate in our minds.

There was one chord which the Senator struck just now to which I vibrated very much when he said "there is always the possibility." Now, this is why I personally, and my party, resist nationalization and nationalized monopoly so strongly—because, when a monopoly is national, when it is the government itself which is running the monopoly, then there is no longer "the possibility." You haven't an appeal then. You haven't the chance of persuading the government to step in and crush those who are attempting to deform the market process, because the self-perpetuating power of government is doing it itself.

I entirely agree with him, and this is something which does run through both our speeches, that you cannot just treat competition as something which will do itself. The very people who run the competitive process, the very private enterprises, if you take your eyes off them for ten seconds, will be finding out some methods of avoiding competition. It's not nice. Nobody likes to be forced into a competitive environment himself.

You've got to have the ground rules. You've got to use the power of the community to see that people are jolly well made to play the game.

SENATOR DOUGLAS: You see how close he is to me, how close? And you all remember Adam Smith's statement: "Gentlemen of the same trade seldom meet together even for merriment or diversion but the meeting turns into a conspiracy against the public and a conspiracy to raise prices."

DR. FRIEDMAN: Yes, as of now, all their meetings are in Washington.

SENATOR DOUGLAS: You only have government ownership in those cases where there was already private monopoly, long continued and relatively unenlightened. This is a point I should have made before: A very large section of industry either is characterized by monopoly, by quasimonopoly or highly-imperfect competition, which, in the nature of the case and from the very laws of demand and cost, tends to restrict output, restrict employment, restrict production.

MR. POWELL: But what do you want to do in such cases? Do you want to nationalize, sir, or do you want to use the power of the state to broaden competition?

SENATOR DOUGLAS: I would like to do two things: Inform the consumer or enable the consumer to be informed and, second, I think we ought to break up some of these huge concerns. I hope the government goes through with its possible suit to break up General

Motors, and breaks up General Motors into four or five different companies based on the divisions of General Motors producing specific cars. I see that this arouses great opposition but, if you believe in the competitive system, why not break it up? I was very pleased when the control of duPont over General Motors was somewhat reduced. I think that was a good move. There are a lot of these concerns which are too big.

But you try to reduce monopoly and introduce competition and all of the people who say they believe in competition will jump on you and say you are antibusiness, that you are a Socialist, that you are a Communist, although this is the exact opposite of socialism and communism.

NORMAN TURE, National Bureau of Economic Research: May I have the liberty of making one passing observation on the point that you have just mentioned?

SENATOR DOUGLAS: Surely.

MR. TURE: I think empirically the observation that monopoly restricts employment and output is really of dubious validity because, in order to maintain it, you would have to say that the strength of monopoly elements in the market in the United States diminishes as we approach a higher degree of resource utilization and increases as unemployment gets larger.

SENATOR DOUGLAS: You mean because of increasing proportions of income being spent for services?

MR. TURE: No, sir. I mean simply to point out that the change in the degree of market concentration is likely to be a process that occurs slowly and over a long period of time, whereas, differences in the rate of resource utilization occur fairly drastically within relatively short periods of time. The coincidence or the correlation between the rate of resource utilization and the degree of market concentration for the economy as a whole is not an obvious one.

But may I turn now to my question, please? It seems to me that, in the interest of not allowing sweetness and light to dominate a rational debate, the key issue on which our speakers divide is whether, given a social option in favor of income redistribution, in favor of reducing the disparity—

SENATOR DOUGLAS: Do you accept that?

MR. TURE: —Oh, sure. In favor of reducing the disparity in the distribution of income and wealth, that this is best achieved through the government participating directly and changing the allocation of money income, as Mr. Powell suggests, or through grants of income in kind, which is in essence many of the things that you were suggesting in your remarks. One approach involves directly a redistribution of income claims but only indirectly a change in the composition of economic activity. The other achieves income redistribution by and large only through changing the composition of economic activity.

If in fact the goal that is being sought is one on which you are both agreed—that is, a certain amount of income redistribution—may I simply put the question to you, sir, would you agree or would you disagree that Professor Powell's approach, which abstracts from direct interference with the market process and which achieves the same amount of change in the distribution of income claims, is a superior one?

SENATOR DOUGLAS: No, I would not say that for many commodities. Take education, for instance. I happen to believe in the system of free public education. But I would not say that schools should be exclusively public: I would permit people to pay for private education if they wished, but I would say that this is a type of expenditure which the community can furnish freely up to the college level to those who want it. I would not have the amount determined according to the income which people have because this would result in a very bad distribution of education. It would mean that the poor really wouldn't have it.

Similarly, I would say that this should apply for police or fire or roads, that you shouldn't have a toll system for the roads and that, as I say, no man should be expected to provide his own Central Park. You can take a whole range. In my first attempt, I went into great detail on both the federal and state budgets—and I had hoped that people who objected might object to certain specific items of that.

Take the general question of war and national defense. I don't believe that national defense can be put upon an individual basis with individuals deciding how much defense they want. This is a decision by the community which the community has to make. If this violates the ethical sense of an individual, he can protest and accept such punishment as the community metes out. But the whole problem of national survival, I think, involves a collective expenditure. I would say health is another factor. There are many things which individuals cannot do individually or even on a voluntary basis mutually. There the state is necessary as an agency.

I think in general it is better to tax surpluses and distribute the surpluses than to increase costs at the margin. I will say that.

I personally would favor family allowances in preference to increasing the minimum wage and I am inclined to think that while the unemployment effects of the minimum wage are greatly exaggerated by Mr. Powell, I believe that they may apply in the case of juveniles. I would not object to lowering the minimum for juveniles in order to induce greater employment.

MR. POWELL: Could we follow the case of education up a little more? I thought this was crucial in the question which was put to us both. Let me take my widow whom, for this purpose, I must provide with a son, of course, of school age. Now, the Senator and I both say we want to supply this family unit with what we would regard as an adequate purchasing power. With this adequate purchasing power, we want to see them go into the market and buy food, clothing, housing, and the rest, and we don't want the market messed up with tickets and rationing for widows and widows' sons.

SENATOR DOUGLAS: All right.

MR. POWELL: We agree on that. But he goes further. He says: "I don't want the same principle applied to education, I don't want an education element included in the income redistributed to the widow." Instead, he says—and perhaps all of us say, but let's examine this for a moment to see why we do it—"I want a system of free and compulsory public education and to which that widow's son will go like any other boy of the same age and attainments."

I suggest a new element has been introduced here, a second community purpose. First, there is the redistributive purpose, that we think it intolerable that any member of the community should be below a given standard of well being. Secondly, however, we have a community purpose to secure a given quantum of education. Were that widow to be provided with an education element in her pension but misspend it by not buying education for her son, we would say: "No, we shall step in, the community will step in, because we have decided as a community that there is to be a certain quantum of education."

So there are two objectives here. First, redistributive, but, second, a community view that, in the community interest, which we are not prepared to leave to individual choice, there must be a given quantum of education.

When you look beneath the surface of a thing like

Medicare or the National Health Service, you find similarly a community decision: "This, dear old citizens, is what you shall jolly well have, this and no less."

Now, as long as they say "this *and no less*," I am not worried. What worries me is when the public system becomes so embracing that it becomes "this and no more," as in the case of the National Health Service. So, I do, with respect, think it is important that we unravel education from the other bundle of purchasables which we wanted to secure to the widow and her son.

SENATOR DOUGLAS: I was always opposed to the Oregon constitutional amendment which forbade the existence of a private school and I was very glad that this was declared unconstitutional by the United States Supreme Court. I believe in complete freedom of the people to use private systems of education, but I would hate to see us merely give cash to parents which they could then use as they wished for any system of education, because I think it would break up the solidarity of the community.

Our society is not as stable as people sometimes assume. When you begin to split up a community on the basis of what I regard as superficial distinctions, I am not certain that the community has the cohesion to survive. This is not a mere theoretical matter. This society is under great strain externally and internally. I would hate to see this spirit of community lost. I think we are losing a great deal of it now and I would hate to see it disappear.

As for ceilings on public services, I am not acquainted with the British system, but certainly under our system of Medicare people can get additional amounts of medical attention and hospital attention, if they wish, or if they want to pay for it. This, of course, somewhat restricts the ability of the poor but they are getting a higher minimum than they would in the absence of these services.

MR. TURE: I wanted to make only one additional observation provoked by your last answer. The question of how society will determine what kind of income redistribution it wants is a terribly thorny question to begin with.

SENATOR DOUGLAS: Certainly.

MR. TURE: And when it is complicated by the fact that some of the decision makers will also insist that there are sufficient externalities with respect to some kinds of activities, that the redistributive process has to involve direct government participation and the provision of income in kind, then the problem I think becomes virtually insoluble. As you just demonstrated, with all due respect—you are very persuasive, I might say—the limit on the number of externalities and the amount of externalities that can be adduced in favor of any such program is very, very far away.

HERBERT STEIN, Brookings Institution: I think that you should ask the same question of Mr. Powell—

though I have begun to wonder, since Mr. Powell's answer about education, whether there is anything more than a literary difference between him and the Senator.

SENATOR DOUGLAS: He is just accidentally a Tory, that's all.

MR. STEIN: I don't hear any principles adduced by which to decide how far we go down this scale, which begins with education and includes parks and smoke and water pollution, other than some preferences. You don't like parks, you prefer symphony halls or something.

But, can you give us any advice on deciding how far we go down the scale in deciding that these are things that the community ought to provide because they are good things? We said the other day they are good things. Last week, I think you took the position you were offering us no prescription but only describing what things were like. Tonight we seem to be a little off that. So I wonder how you would, if at all, distinguish your attitude towards this question from Senator Douglas'?

MR. POWELL: I don't think I have resiled from what I said last week. You are back again to what was the main part of the debate which followed Senator Douglas' original paper. Granted that as a community we wish to secure a given quantum and quality of education, as a minimum, on what objective standards do we determine how much that should be?

My answer is: There are no such standards; in the

nature of things you can only discover an answer by a kind of circular process, by looking at a society and finding out what that society has regarded as a community good, something which they will act to secure, regardless of the other consequences. In fact, the limit is contained, roughly and readily, in those words, "regardless of the other consequences."

Take education. Education is an unlimited good but we all realize that there is a point beyond which it is unacceptable for community decision to push up the quantum of education, to increase the fraction of the community's activity that is devoted to imparting and absorbing education. This is subjective. I can imagine a community which decided that 50 percent of the total effort of the community should be devoted to imparting and receiving educational instruction. And how could you argue with them, if they were happy with it?

SENATOR DOUGLAS: May I say, I think in this country we have reached certain very definite standards on education. In the main we believe that up to 16 years of age boys and girls should spend the predominant portion of the year in education. When I was growing up, it was 14 years, and in many states it was 12 years. But we have pushed on now. I think the real question is: Are you going to say we should go back to 14 or go back to 12? I don't think so. I think modern life is so complicated and really the possible joy of education is so great that the 16-year limit is not an unwise one.

DR. FRIEDMAN: I would love to take on this argument with Mr. Powell about the community, which I find very hard to accept. I think of us as achieving our individual objectives and I am afraid his road is not a road I would want to follow.

But I really want to go back to Senator Douglas and public education, because I believe that the real issue is not: Do we want children in school up to 16 years. I think the real issue is: How does this country, how do we as individuals, arrange our affairs so people get good schooling, the best schooling they possibly can, with the greatest opportunity and the most diversity?

Now, it seems to me again, Senator, that you are applying a double standard. If any private industry had performed as miserably as our public education system has performed in achieving the objectives that you and I would like to have it achieve, I do not believe you would be saying, "Well, it is only an accident."

If I ask myself, in what respect is a poor resident of a Negro slum in Chicago most disadvantaged, it seems to me that there is hardly any commodity with respect to which he is more disadvantaged than he is with respect to public schooling. It seems to me the reason for that is that we have insisted not only on compelling him to go to school, not only on financing schooling, in his case poorly—in fact, we profess to give equal schooling opportunities to all children but there is no doubt that the amount of money being spent per head on him is less than the amount of money being spent per head in the suburbs—not only do we do those two things but we insist on having the government run the school, and it runs schools very badly. It seems to me that the crucial issue that we should face is this: Is it not at least arguable that the system in which you introduce competition for schooling, in which, insofar as you are going to finance schooling, you give family heads money and a voucher for schooling and let them spend it—isn't it at least arguable that that would give you better schooling?

I must confess I would go further. I personally see absolutely no reason whatsoever why we should finance schooling for the citizens of Flossmoor, Illinois, or Scarsdale, New York, through tax methods. I see no reason why we shouldn't, in those cases, just tell them there is compulsory schooling up to age 16, just as you are compelled to keep your houses in a shape in which they are not a threat to your neighbors. The reason there is compulsory schooling is not to help your children, we should say, but to prevent your children from hurting the rest of the community. Then let them finance it out of their own pocket.

Now, is there something antidemocratic in that approach and isn't that something we ought to learn from our experience?

SENATOR DOUGLAS: If you universalize this, if you merely give a certificate and allow people to choose whichever school they will, you fragment the quality of education. What you will get then will be a division of education, not merely between Protestants and Catholics but orthodox Jews, Methodists, Unitarians, various groups. You will get a whole series of separate schools.

I don't believe that you get greater efficiency that way. It may seem that what I am advocating is a type of monopoly. It is not that; it allows differentiation but it provides a common basis for the great majority. I am not going to join the current attack on free public education. I think it has done extremely well considering its difficulties. The difficulties are obvious. Today a deprived section of the public, formerly confined to the rural districts of the South or the mountains of the Appalachians, have moved in upon the cities with all of the cultural disadvantages of a century or centuries. We are now inheriting them. It is asking a little bit too much that the schools shall in a short period of time overcome all of this. I don't want to fragment this effort.

If you go on from education into other things, how can individuals individually provide for parks? How can they provide for sewers? How can they provide for water supply? There are many things which have to be done collectively if they are done at all, and no man can carry on his back his own sewer system, so to speak.

MR. POWELL: Nor his railway train.

SENATOR DOUGLAS: That is right.

MR. POWELL: Yes, but that is provided through the market.

SENATOR DOUGLAS: Not entirely, not entirely.

A VOICE: It· would be better if it were.

MR. POWELL: I am not sure that I am happy about Professor Friedman's intervention. I think the reply to it from the Senator did show clearly and candidly that he is pursuing a non-educational object in his educational policy; namely, a national policy, a policy of increasing homogeneity. If he were told that private schooling would result in equal attainments, he would nevertheless say, "Yes, but there is something else I want as well, which I regard as important to this country and, therefore, I want an education system which will give that as well." In other words, he has a second community objective and he is entitled to have that. But I do think that Professor Friedman overlooked the difficulty which perhaps I could bring out by substituting the word "clothing" for "education" in his question.

He said the only thing we are worried about—the only thing he was worried about—was how the people get the best education they possibly can. Now, when we say: How do people get the best clothing they possibly can? we all agree, I imagine, with his answer: Well, let them go and buy it and, if there is a small minority who can't buy it, we will redistributively give them the income with which to buy it.

Now, let us take "clothing" out and put "education" back. He says we'll just tell everybody "You've got to educate your children until blank years of age" and let them get on with it. If there is a small minority that hasn't got enough to pay school fees, all right, we'll give them a subvention, we'll redistribute to the necessary extent. Right?

I am sure you could do that, if you required elementary education of a certain standard. Probably you might get away with it, if you required education up to, say, the age of 12. But there does come a point at which the conflict between the choice of the individual in laying out his income and the obligation placed upon him by the community, which has decided that people ought to be at school until 16, becomes intolerable. You escape from this intolerable conflict by the combination of compulsion with public provision.

I do think that the Professor is making it easy for himself when he picks the suburbs, the tiny minorities where self-evidently those placed under compulsion would pay the market fees, and then leaves it at that.

DR. FRIEDMAN: Sure, I would be glad to answer, because I really think that this is a distinction without a difference at the moment. I was citing the suburbs because I wanted to argue that I don't accept the view that there is something universal about the desirability of the governmental-financed schools. I quite agree that for the large-city groups or the non-tiny minority, that there are large groups for which it is desirable to handle education, not for the reasons you give but for other reasons, through vouchers and providing the finance.

The thing I would like to emphasize is that as our nation becomes more affluent and as we have a better distribution of income, I would like to see a system under which the size of what you now call tiny minorities increases, where the people do provide for themselves. I personally, as a matter of fact, am not at all sure that the argument even for compulsory schooling at that level is at all as strong as it is under different circumstances in other kinds of societies. I know the book by Edward West of Britain which suggests that in Britain in the absence of compulsory schooling in the nineteenth century there was an enormously rapid expansion of private provision of schooling for large numbers of people in the community.

I was just taking it for granted, for the sake of the argument, that we were talking about compulsory schooling. I was accepting the finance of schooling and then asking: How can we achieve this objective best? I am not sure you would really want to differ on the desirability of shifting away from a system under which we do this through the state purse into a system under which each individual family provides for it out of his own purse. Would you object to that as an objective?

MR. POWELL: I am sure that there is a correlation between what people would in any case do—for example, about education—and the general standard of living and other things about a community. But if, as we have done recently in Britain in university education, you take a community decision for community reasons, such as: "We are going to double the quantum of university education," then I don't believe you can use the method of compulsion plus the market to achieve that end. You have to step in the direction of what I called in my paper specific government. This exposes the point which I have been trying to make over and over again, that where you have decided upon a quantum you are determined to have, you are led to obtain that by specific action. It will rarely produce itself spontaneously.

KIRKLEY COULTER, Senate Antitrust Subcommittee: My question is for Mr. Powell. If the question is how big government should be, there seems to be an implicit assumption here that the size of government is somehow controllable by the community, however we define this. The doubt in my mind is that we can actually keep this thing under control. I have a feeling that some parts of it at least seem to grow of their own momentum. We create agencies to accomplish a purpose and they seem to live on and on. There is no mechanism in this whole institutional structure for bringing an agency to an end. So I raise the question: What is the social machinery that we have to limit government from growing of its own motion or, perhaps to phrase it the other way: May it not be the case that there is a conflict between the decision machine— that is the community will, however we define that—

and these internal urges that exist in the government to grow?

MR. POWELL: The only mechanism I can offer is opinion. In my paper last week I drew attention to the fact that there had been periods in which opinion had brought about an actual reduction of government, when it was commonly believed that the solution to almost any problem lay in the reduction of government, just as today the common opinion is that the solution to any problem must lie in an extension of government.

Now, I don't know how you chemically produce the change in the weather, this sort of change in the weather, although I know that politicians are supposed to be weather makers.

The best, in fact, that I can do is go around talking, if haply this might strike a spark in a sufficient number of bosoms—male and female—so that somehow a reversal of the trend takes place.

I drew attention again in my paper to the fact that there were perhaps detectable certain pendulum or wave movements between prejudice in favor of government and the prejudice against government. I can't help you more than that. *Quis custodiet?*

SENATOR DOUGLAS: I would like to ask Mr. Coulter: What is there in the structure of private monopoly which restricts its expansion? Mr. Coulter seems to be greatly opposed to the expansion of government. How about the expansion of General Motors?

of duPont? What about the expansion of many of these companies or alliances or mergers?

MR. COULTER: It does not have the power of sovereignty to impose its decisions on the public.

SENATOR DOUGLAS: Now wait a minute. It has the sovereignty—

MR. COULTER: It has great power but not the power of sovereignty.

SENATOR DOUGLAS: Sovereignty is in reality merely power. You read John W. Burgess, who was our expert on sovereignty, and you will find he essentially defines sovereignty as power. And they have economic sovereignty in many cases. It is only an exceptional Ralph Nader who can take them on.

MR. COULTER: To take your case, sir, if the government makes a decision duPont cannot overrule it. But, if duPont and General Motors make a decision, the government can take them into court and force a divestiture.

SENATOR DOUGLAS: Yes, under somewhat peculiar terms. But I would also say that this is a very eloquent argument for the government splitting up General Motors. I would expect you to favor this now.

RICHARD MURPHY, staff of Senator Hugh Scott: At the risk of being accused of partisan politics, I doubt if the government is going to break up General Motors, as long as the President's Club remains in existence.

SENATOR DOUGLAS: We probably get corrupted like the others, only not corrupted as much.

WILLIAM COLMAN, Commission on Intergovernmental Relations: Mr. Powell, accepting the qualifications that you made about public education, would you generally favor the substitution of a guaranteed annual income in lieu of the provision by government of various services, welfare, health, housing, etc., to the people who need them?

MR. POWELL: Yes, except that there are some such services or needs which are not regularly recurrent but are intermittent. In those cases I think you may well envisage the income as being laid out, not in the purchase of those services as we envisage it being laid out— in food, heat, lighting, and so on—but in the purchase of security for meeting them, i.e., enough to pay the appropriate insurance premium. With that qualification, my answer to your question is: Yes.

DR. FRIEDMAN: I just want to come back to Senator Douglas on this question of what there is that controls the monopoly. I would have supposed that his answer and my answer would be the greed of other human beings. I would suppose that the real reason why he and I should be in favor of having government stay out of this business is because, once you get government into it, you keep other human beings from breaking down these monopolies.

There is an old saying that if you want to catch a thief, you set a thief. If you want to catch a capitalist, you set a capitalist.

It seems to me the greatest argument for free enter-

prise is not what General Motors calls free enterprise
and not what Roger Blough calls free enterprise, but
what Senator Douglas and I call free enterprise. It is
the only system which keeps the capitalist from having
too much power.

SENATOR DOUGLAS: This assumes that the potential competitor can start on comparatively even
terms. But there is such a thing, of course, as the advantage of size. A huge concern, which might ultimately
be ineffective, can, nevertheless, crush small concerns
by this sheer factor of size. This was demonstrated over
and over again in the growth of the so-called trusts.
You only have to read Ida Tarbell's history of the
Standard Oil Company and others to see that. This
was why we passed the Clayton Act of 1914. We sometimes forget the Clayton Act.

No, positive action of government is frequently
needed in order to obtain competition and also, I would
say, to set the ethical minimum, or minima below which
competition should not go.

MR. POWELL: I agree with that about the necessity
for government policing, but I do think there may be
some confusion in this notion of large undertakings
crushing out potential competitors by sheer size.

First of all, we tend to think of a potential competitor
as a little man. But the potential competitor is very
often a big man. Where sheer size is necessary for the
minimum undertaking, the competition which a large
but relatively inefficient undertaking may have to fear

is the entry into its own field of something very big, already operating in another field, which may have billions, certainly millions of dollars at its disposal, for putting into the fight.

Secondly, the whole history—certainly in Britain and it must be the same here—of the industrial pattern in the last 20 years has shown case after case of the individual who found a little niche, a little corner, where the big enterprise was not giving the service which he could give; and who clung on there like a limpet in a hole in the rock. Then he grewed and grewed and grewed.

And in the end, size didn't prevail because the little grew to be big. I don't believe there is anything in the mere size of an undertaking which protects it against competition unless, of course, you mean through crushing it out by malpractice. There you have to use the law just as you use it against forgery or theft.

DR. HARRISS: I want to make this as unemotional as possible. You are talking about government without, I would say, adequate account of the cost of government. Taxes in the United States this year will be about $1,000 per capita, about $5,000 for a family of five.

Now, we talk about redistribution, but is government a reasonably efficient instrument for redistributing these amounts? The taxes on poorer people total pretty high. We have known that. This is not a new thing. This goes on year after year. I don't know what the market would do, but certainly large government is not, I would submit, a markedly efficient instrument for achieving the kind of redistribution that we would like.

SENATOR DOUGLAS: Oh, I would agree with you. I have never felt that the general property tax was an equitable tax. I don't like sales taxes.

DR. HARRISS: But the corporation income tax takes more from poor people than the sales taxes.

SENATOR DOUGLAS: In what way?

DR. HARRISS: Assuming that half of it is shifted to the consumer.

SENATOR DOUGLAS: I thought that profits were a surplus and not—

DR. HARRISS: No.

SENATOR DOUGLAS: —and not a cost, but we could get into quite a discussion on that point. I would like to have a unitary tax on incomes and I confess to being something of a heretic in believing that a special tax on land values would be very appropriate.

DR. HARRISS: I couldn't agree with you more. Then why haven't we? This is an old idea, well known.

SENATOR DOUGLAS: You see, it is so hard for us to make our opinions, sensible opinions, prevail when we have such powerful antagonists.

MR. POWELL: I think, with great respect, Professor Harriss misuses the expressions "redistribute," "redistributive" in the context of his question. Surely only a tiny fraction of the tax per head to which he referred in the United States is applied to redistributive purposes, i.e., to the supplementation of the purchasing power of individuals or families.

Surely far the greater part of it is devoted to community purposes—general, not individual—such as promoting a supersonic airliner or the race to the moon or the war in Vietnam or whatever it may be. I don't think this is redistribution. But, using "redistribution" in this correct sense, is the state an efficient redistributive instrument? The answer must be: Maybe not, but there is no other. If you want redistribution, this is in essence a community decision which can only be carried out through the channels of the community. You can tinker around with them and you can shake them so as to get the process done, as you judge, more efficiently. But there is no alternative to the mechanism of the community, if redistribution is your object.

SENATOR DOUGLAS: You see how much more intelligent the British Conservatives are than the American conservatives?

DR. HARRISS: The Senator and Dr. Ture got on the redistribution approach, but you don't need big government to get as much redistribution as we would want.

MR. TURE: May I object to that at this point? I have just jotted down an observation or question. The discussion has focused this evening very substantially on the questions of the income-redistribution function of government, but the question on which this debate is supposedly organized is: How Big Should Government Be? I don't know that anyone in this room will posit that the size of government is properly the function of the extent of income redistribution to be sought.

MR. POWELL: That is only one minor activity.

MR. TURE: That's right.

DR. FRIEDMAN: But it seems to me, in answer to what Mr. Powell says, that the question cannot be answered in terms of: Do we seek redistribution or do we not. Or, to go back, it cannot be answered in the terms that Senator Douglas put it, that there are the people who are the powerful enemies; that we must persuade the people to be enlightened. It seems to me the question is a different one, one that is really implicit in Mr. Powell's position earlier. In my opinion, it is no accident that when you have a big government it turns out to produce inequality rather than equality. That is the nature of the beast.

The question one should ask is: What is wrong with the system? What are the political principles and rules upon which you can avoid these outcomes? I don't believe it is by trying to enlighten the people on percentage depletion by itself, or on the particulars of tariffs or quotas. I believe it is along the line of Cobden and Bright, by having the people recognize that they must adopt a general presumption that the state stays out of a wide range of things. Unless you have that general presumption of nonintervention, it seems to me that Senator Douglas and the noble and glorious people who follow him are doomed to failure in trying to hold back the special interests whose power in the political process seems to me to be larger than it is in the economic process. The only way we can stop them is by all of us banding together on the principle, so far as possible: Let us alone.

I really am in favor of the laissez faire principle of the original Cobden and Bright as the only safeguard against these malefactors of great wealth whom Senator Douglas has so nobly opposed.

JAMES STEINER, National Chamber of Commerce: May we ask Mr. Powell to describe in some more detail, if he will, what he does to change attitudes? You spoke of this both last week and this week, and yet you say so many of these decisions are made by introducing factors which are incommensurable. So I am asking: What's believable? What's good or bad or what's meaningful? And tell us more about this psychology of changing attitudes, if you can't give us quantum relationships that are economic in establishing reasons for limiting government.

MR. POWELL: I will let you into a secret, a politician's secret. Fortunately I can do so because there is no secret so close as that which people do not wish to believe. And people do not wish to believe the arcana of the politicians. Therefore the arcana of the politicians remain inviolate today as they have been through the centuries. Nevertheless, I will spread out my goods and you can disbelieve them.

We know nothing, we politicians, even about the way in which so simple and overt a matter as votes at an election can be influenced. We don't even know what happens at an election, let alone how to influence the votes of an election. How much less can we have any notion of the relationship between our behavior and those movements of opinion which are *ex post facto* observed or believed to be observed by the historians.

So you ask me what do I do. I will tell you what I do, all day long, year in and year out, as a politician. I sit in the hedge and sing. You will recognize my reference to Luther's Reformation hymn. One day the dawn perhaps comes and I perhaps am the bird that heralded the dawn. But it is not for me to know. Only for me to know that this is the song that is in my heart and that this I must sit in the hedge and sing, if perchance the dawn might come. I shall not cause the dawn. I shall simply be one of the many twitters and trills that herald its coming. However, maybe it ain't going to dawn after all.

SENATOR DOUGLAS: We are getting near the end and I don't know how appropriate this poetry is, but when my friend was quoting those lines based on Luther I thought of William Blake's:

I shall not rest from mental strife
Nor shall my sword sleep in my hand
Till we have built Jerusalem
In England's green and pleasant land.

That's what some of us are trying to do here in this country.

MR. POWELL: You must come and do it in England.

FOOTNOTES

FIRST LECTURE

[1] U.S. Bureau of the Census, *Government Finances in 1965-66*. Series g.F. 13, 1967, p. 2.